When Lions Roar
How to Tame a Wild Tongue

DAWN MOORING

Cover design by artist Jon Krause.

CONTENTS

PROLOGUE

What do you see when look at the cover of this book? Are you the lion holding someone captive with the power of your mouth, your roar? Or are you the person desperately desiring to escape the snare of the lion's mouth?

Oh, the power of the mouth and the words that flow from it...

Most people fall into one of two camps – the wordy or the quiet. The "wordies" often bless others with wisdom and principles which encourage and instruct. Yet sometimes their words can be destructive, doing way more damage than good. The quiet, or "less wordies," hold back on their verbal outpourings for the greater good. Their silence can bless. Their silence can also be profoundly destructive.

What does God, our MOUTHMAKER, have to say about the mouth and what flows from it?

This book is a valiant effort of combing the pages of Scripture to search out how God instructs the ebb and flow of our words. This compilation of verses on the mouth, tongue, lips and the way we speak will enlighten us about honoring God, others, and even ourselves when our jaws open and the sentences begin. Lessons for life come from the very mouth of our Lord and as a result should flow from our mouths as well.

Perhaps like me, you are desperate for accountability with your oratory vehicle! You long for your mouth to be an instrument God uses to build His kingdom. In the pages that follow, there is great counsel for growth. Heed the advice of the MOUTHMAKER, our all wise God.

"Let the words of my mouth and the meditation of my heart be acceptable in your sight, O Lord, my Rock and my Redeemer" Psalm 10:14 (ESV).

ACKNOWLEDGMENTS

The first Scripture I ever memorized was Psalm 100. Little did I know years would pass before I understood verse 3, "It is He who has made us, and not we ourselves." God made me and gave me the ability to write. Writing helps me see God, myself, and others more clearly. He has allowed me to see myself as both lion and the lion's prey. I am grateful. Without His intervention I would not be able to serve Him or others. My prayer is that He would use this book to make something beautiful out of all our suffering.

To my husband, Mark – Thank you for loving me when the lion emerged out of me. By your loving and patient example you have shown me a better way to handle conflict.

To my family and friends – Your desire for my growth has led you to pray for me when I asked, and most likely, even when I didn't ask. You've seen my darkest side and prayed for the Spirit of God to break through. My mom always said, "It's always the darkest before the dawn." Perhaps she was a bit prophetic in naming me.

To my pastor, Johnny Hunt – I have heard you speak about your lion side. I thank God for changing you and showing others the lion can be crucified.

To Grace Ministries International – I am forever indebted to your ministry, especially Scott Brittin. You showed me my identity was in Christ, not what I did or what others did to me.

To the lions in my life – You have been placed in my life at various times. Most likely you aren't even reading this book. Believe it or not, I am thankful for you. You have caused me to cry out to God. You have shown me how destructive a life of roaring can be. You were placed in my life as a catalyst for change. Praise the Lord!

THE FOUNTAIN

When arrogant words are followed by harsh actions, the destiny's end is never good.

Living in Atlanta has its perks. When friends and family visit, there are plenty of exciting attractions to explore. One of my favorites is the World of Coca-Cola. It's not the fountain of youth, but the "Taste It!" beverage lounge can certainly invigorate your taste buds. Flowing freely from a base fountain are 100 + variations of Coca-Cola, formulated for the unique palates of people around the globe. To me, some of the flavors are tasty; others definitely are not.

The Coca-Cola base fountain is where each taste variation begins; it holds the pure version of Coke. If that version were to become contaminated, all variations would be tainted.

What flows from our mouths has a base as well. Individuals may speak identical words of advice, warning, compliment, or criticism; however, the heart from which they flow impacts reception. If the base of the fountain is filled with love, words of advice, criticism, or caution, are palatable, even if they are hard to receive. If bitterness oozes from an individual, others may immediately recoil, even from a compliment. When someone's fountain is filled with anger or jealousy, acidic words can flow like hot lava, scalding others, perhaps causing permanent damage.

So the question we must ask ourselves is, *what flows from the base of my fountain?*

The book of Exodus is filled with wisdom about the importance of knowing the answer to this question. Remember when baby Moses was placed in a floating basket? The sovereign God of the universe had a plan; He knew Pharaoh's daughter would find that precious cargo. Moses went from a floating basket to a grand palace and became a well-educated young man, fluent in both Hebrew and Arabic.

We learn in Acts 7:22 that Moses was "mighty in word and deeds." But one not-so-mighty deed was the murder of an Egyptian who was abusing a Hebrew slave. When confronted about the murder, Moses ran. His confidence evaporated, and fear became the base of his fountain. Forty years later, when Moses saw the burning bush from which God began to speak, he was afraid to look. When God instructed Moses to tell Pharaoh to free the Israelites, fear gushed from the hole in Moses' heart. He tried to explain that he wasn't the man for the job because he was "slow of speech and slow of tongue." (Exodus 4:10) God didn't buy the baloney Moses was trying to sell.

I've tried to sell the Lord some lame excuses. Countless times I've reminded Him just how busy I was (as if He didn't know my schedule). When He's prompted me to visit a neighbor and invite them to a church function, fear coupled with procrastination led me down a path of excuses.

In Exodus 4:11-12, the Lord asks Moses, "Who has made man's mouth? Who makes him mute, or deaf, or seeing, or blind? Is it not I, the Lord? Now therefore go, and I will be with your mouth and teach you what you shall speak." God promised to replace Moses' base of fear with a fountain of words that would stream from the Almighty God of the universe!

You'd think Moses would have exhaled a sigh of relief. Nope. In Exodus 4:13 he responds, "Please send someone else." Rather than edit Moses totally out of the story, as you and I might have done, God allowed Aaron, Moses' brother, to partner with him to confront Pharaoh. God promised to be the mouthpiece for both imperfect men. And He delivered.

CONFRONTING AN AGGRESSIVE LION

When the base of a fountain is the Lord, mountains move. And Pharaohs, too. But that doesn't mean they won't first put up a bloodthirsty fight!

In Exodus 5:1(ESV), Moses and Aaron stood before Pharaoh and delivered the message: "This is what the Lord, the God of Israel, says: 'Let my people go, so that they may hold a festival to me in the wilderness." How's that for getting straight to the point?

Pharaoh, who was likely seated on his throne, looking down on Moses and Aaron in more ways than one, responds with a definite sarcastic growl in verse two: "Who is the Lord that I should obey him and let Israel go? I do not know the Lord, and I will not let Israel go."

Because Pharaoh was not a follower of the one true God, the message Moses and Aaron delivered ticked him off royally. Anger flowed from his fountain. He was totally oblivious to the fact that the message the brothers delivered was not a *suggestion* but a firm *command* of the Lord. Pharaoh immediately pounced, reacting with harsh words and cruel actions, making the work of the Israelite slaves even harder. "That same day Pharaoh gave this order to the slave drivers and overseers in charge of the people: "You are no longer to supply the people with straw for making bricks; let them go and gather their own straw. But require them to make the same number of bricks as before; don't reduce the quota. They are lazy; that is why they are crying out, 'Let us go and sacrifice to our God.' Make the work harder for the people so that they keep working and pay no attention to lies" Exodus 5:6-9(NIV).

When the base of our fountain is impure, we are likely to react with our words too. There is a difference between *reacting* and *responding*. *Reacting* with words may cause us to speak in opposition to an influencing statement or conversation. One definition of *reaction* is *a change in atomic nuclei*. Perhaps this is where the phrase "blowing up in a conversation" was coined! *Reacting* is a knee-jerk action caused by stimuli. It's a gush of words and toxic emotions. *Responding* is radically different; it stops and draws a calming breath before speaking.

When I read Pharaoh's verbal reaction in Exodus 5, I detect a definite power struggle. In all likelihood, he had heard of the God the Israelites worshipped. He lived in a palace, not under a rock! The God of Abraham, Isaac, and Jacob had quite a reputation. Pride fused to an obsession with power and a need for control, likely propelled Pharaoh to act as a vicious lion backed into a corner. He began to roar — loudly with teeth bared and claws extended. To be on the receiving end of such fierce aggression would make the stoutest man tremble. David, the Psalmist, clearly understood the danger such a lion represented. He cried out to God in Psalm 22:21: "Save me from the lion's mouth…" God's people needed deliverance from the brutal lion named Pharaoh because his roar was getting louder by the minute.

I grew up in a house of lions. Roaring and knee jerk responses were the norm for our family. While there is not a gene for toxic communication, what was passed down in the way of conflict resolution, was certainly less than healthy. I had six sisters and we shared tight quarters. Fights erupted daily. As children we resolved matters the way we were taught. Screaming, crying, and negative barbs were the weapons we fought with. Later in life I realized poor communication skills, coupled with unhealthy fears, poised me as an intimidator. On the turn of a dime I roared like Pharaoh, and quaked fearfully as Moses the next.

SOUND EFFECTS

Have you ever heard a lion roar? The terrifying sound can be heard as far as five miles! What makes a lion roar?

"According to the Bible, a lion roars when it

3

has prey in sight. The question is asked in Amos 3:4: 'Will a lion roar in the forest, when he hath no prey?' The context of the verse is that, no, he will not. The lion's roar brings fear to its prey, thus Amos 3:8 says, 'The lion has roared, who will not fear?' The roaring of the lion when he has prey causes fear in the victim, and this fear makes escaping harder for the victim and thus aids the lion in capturing his food. 'Their roaring shall be like a lion, they shall roar like young lions: yea, they shall roar, and lay hold of the prey, and shall carry it away safe, and none shall deliver it' " Isaiah 5:29.i

I have been the trembling prey of a human lion. If you, too, have been prey, then you understand the paralyzing fear it produces. A feeling of helplessness engulfs you. The desire to fight back is trumped by the terror of repercussion that may ensue. The Bible warns us not to argue with a hot tempered man or we may just lose our lives. Hot tempers need time to cool down. A wise person waits for a drop in the temperature.

In Exodus 5:9, we see how Pharaoh roared and refused to allow the Israelites time off to worship God. He called them lazy liars! He pushed more work on them, had them beaten, and demanded they ignore the words of Moses and Aaron, essentially telling the Israelites to ignore God and listen to him instead. It seems Pharaoh's fountain was also filled with no small amount of deadly arrogance. And stubbornness. Lots of stubbornness.

Pharaoh would one day drown in his arrogant words. 1 Samuel 2:3 (ESV) warns, "Talk no more so very proudly, let not arrogance come from your mouth; for the LORD is a God of knowledge, and by him actions are weighed."

There is weightiness to words. Pharaoh was not careful with his. We must be extremely careful with ours. This powerful man directed the course of human lives with his words. We have the power to do the same with ours. People turn left or right because of what we say or even because of our silence, sometimes because of misinterpreted silence. When someone perceives our quietness as disapproval they may try harder to win favor, or relinquish even trying at all. Silence isn't always golden.

SIGNIFICANT INFORMATION

As we journey through the book of Exodus and witness the 10 horrific plagues God used to get Pharaoh's attention, note the significant information supplied. God told Moses and Aaron precisely what to say to Pharaoh. "King Powerhouse" didn't like what the brothers had to say, but their fountain base was the words of the Lord. They were careful to speak only what they had been told to speak. And every word of God came to pass.

There was a time in my life when God prompted me to speak to an individual about a contentious situation. I can relate to the fear of Moses. This powerhouse of a person was my boss. Demeaning looks and condescending barbs were his daily ritual. I'd reached my threshold of emotional pain, and realized I needed to either confront or quit. As a single mom, confronting was my only hope for a better ending. Before the meeting began, I begged God to speak through me. I wanted His words to come out of my mouth, no more, no less. After my holy pow-wow ended, I waited. I wasn't fired. There was a gradual change in the office. Much to my surprise, this boss apologized to me years later. I am thankful I spoke only what God had revealed to me

Listen to this instruction of God to the prophet Jeremiah regarding speaking, "Thus says the LORD: Stand in the court of the LORD's house, and speak to all the cities of Judah that come to worship in the house of the LORD all the words that I command you to speak to them; do not hold back a word." Jeremiah 26:2 (KJV)

God knows we have the human tendency to ad-lib. That is why a pure fountain base is so vital. A pure base will help us stick to the script and keep a straight face. Ad- libbing from an impure base will lead to facial contortions and wordy distortions of the worst kind. I confess I have been guilty of those things! Ever thought of totally speaking your mind and telling someone off? First, practice in front of the mirror. Not a pretty sight!

I can only imagine Pharaoh's facial expressions as he heard the exact words of the Lord from Moses and Aaron. Pharaoh took orders from no one. He refused to be told how to rule his empire. His heart was evil; his fountain rancid. His words and actions followed suit. Matthew 12:24 (ESV) explains this type of polluted fountain: "You brood of vipers! How can you speak good when you are evil? For out of the abundance of the heart the mouth speaks." Evil spewed from Pharaoh's fountain with every word he spoke.

As you can tell by now, I'm not giving Pharaoh any slack. I know those who have the gift of mercy may think, *He was once a mama's sweet baby boy. Surely there's some good in there.* So, I will try to show a bit of mercy. Here goes: Pharaoh looked great on the outside. His exterior was grand — robes made with golden threads and a crown of gold and ivory. But the opulent wardrobe of this powerful leader could not cover his gross inferiority complex. Most people who boast and huff and puff do so to cover up fear and insecurities. I wonder if, down deep, Pharaoh feared that what he most revered could be easily destroyed by the God the Israelites worshipped.

Throughout the book of Exodus, Pharaoh's heart is repeatedly described as *hard* or *hardened.* This man, like each one of us, was endowed by God with a free will, or the freedom to make choices apart from God. When Pharaoh locked into his arrogance, pride, and stubbornness, God allowed those sins to reach their maximum capacity for danger. Exodus 7:14 tells us, "The Lord said to Moses, 'Pharaoh's heart is unyielding; he refuses to let the people go.'" In Exodus 7:22, this hardening is confirmed: "…Pharaoh's heart became hard; he would not listen to Moses and Aaron, just as the Lord had said."

One of the Hebrew meanings for *hard* is to *grow stout.* To swell in one's pride is a recipe for disaster. Listen to some of God's thoughts and actions against the proud: *He smites them. They will be brought low. He will not endure them. He rebukes them. They will be ashamed. He keeps them at a distance. He will destroy their house. They are an abomination to Him.*

God doesn't view arrogance as a misdemeanor; it's a major offense. The words of an arrogant person are offensive to others. Most of all, they offend God.

A well-known quote warns, "Be careful of your thoughts, for your thoughts become your words. Be careful of your words, for your words become your actions. Be careful of your actions, for your actions become your habits. Be careful of your habits, for your habits become your character. Be careful of your character, for your character becomes your destiny."[ii] When arrogant words are followed by harsh actions, the destiny's end is never good. Pharaoh's words and destiny were both swallowed up in the end. He lost everything because he refused to listen to words that meant everything.

As for Moses and Aaron, they saw firsthand the blessings of speaking only what the Lord had told them. They reaped the benefits of faithful words followed by faithful actions.

James 3:10-13(ESV) makes it clear, "From the same mouth come blessing and cursing. My brothers, these things ought not to be so. Does a spring pour forth from the same opening both fresh and salt water? Can a fig tree, my brothers, bear olives, or a grapevine produce figs? Neither can a salt pond yield fresh water. Who is wise and understanding among you? By his good conduct let him show his works in the meekness of wisdom."

When Moses and Aaron stood before Pharaoh and the children of Israel, their fountain produced only fresh water. Their works were done in meekness and wisdom. In Exodus 14 they witnessed one of the greatest miracles in the Bible – the parting of the Red Sea. As they were faithful to impart fresh water from their fountain, they watched a huge body of salt water part before their eyes. When the salty, arrogant Pharaoh attempted to follow the Israelites, he got a taste of his own medicine. God "unparted" the sea when Pharaoh reached the point of no return. Some people end up eating their words; Pharaoh had to drink his.

LIFESTYLE CHANGE

Over the years, I've limited my beverage intake to water and coffee. Raised in the South, my liquid mainstays for years were sweet iced tea and Diet Coke. I rarely drank water — until I discovered the negative impact impure substances had on my kidneys. I switched to eight daily glasses of water. I couldn't believe the difference in how I felt! I had more energy. I felt as if I had recuperated from a long illness. I never realized the impact those toxins had on my body. Don't get me wrong; I'm no health nut, but I lean toward good health. Drinking pure water has been the best lifestyle change I've ever made.

Why am elaborating on this small detail of my life? It's a simple analogy: Garbage in, garbage out. If you feast off negativity, vulgarity, profanity, and all the other ugly "itys," your verbal output will sound the same. What your fountain is filled with, is what it dispenses. What immediately flows from your fountain when you are irritated? The book of James makes it clear that a spring can't pour out fresh and salty water at the same time.

The song "All My Fountains" talks about the importance of one's fountain being in God alone. God's love is Living Water, flowing in and through us like a river from heaven, not a trickle. His love can flood our souls to the point of overflow.

Is your fountain base pure Living Water that flows from God through His Son, Jesus Christ? Jesus represents the living water that quenches all thirst. When we are filled with this hydrating potion we dispense, even overflow His love. What about you – does love flow through your words? Is it time for a lifestyle change?

Psalm 19:14 (ESV) is a great verse for such a change: "Let the words of my mouth and the meditation of my heart be acceptable in your sight, O LORD, my rock and my redeemer."

MOMENTS IN THE MIRROR

CHAPTER 1

1. What flows from the base of your fountain? If you could peer through a scope to discover the stimulus for your words and conversations, what do you think you'd find?

2. Like Moses' initial response to God, do you speak from fear? Or does fear silence you?

3. Pharaoh achieved a great title, but he was not a great man. Perhaps his title went to his head. No crown would have been large enough to wrap around all the arrogant, puffed up thoughts that spewed from him in words and deeds. Ever been guilty of thinking too highly of yourself? Has pride ever slipped out in your conversations?

4. Are you a reactor or a responder?

5. Are you afraid of others? Or are others afraid of you?

6. If you had to "eat your words" today would they taste good?

Take a moment to pause as you reflect on your answers to these questions. If you have a nagging sensation that there's room for growth in your verbal skills (and we're not talking grammar here), stop right now and pray. Ask God to purify your fountain. His mercies are new every morning. Great is His faithfulness. Look at how many chances the Lord gave Pharaoh to change his ways!

GREAT START, POOR FINISH

If we chose constant grumbling and use others for verbal target practice, that's cesspool living.

Over the years, we've all had heroes — sports figures, actors, authors, family members, religious leaders — who, like Humpty Dumpty, had a great fall. We shake our heads in amazement and wonder, *How could they? Why would they?* It's easy to think we would never do what others have done or say what others have said. But every one of us could make a decision that would tarnish the way we finish our journey.

Let's pick back up with Moses. He and the Israelites looked in the rearview mirror and watched Pharaoh's army disappear into the Red Sea. God showed His power — and Moses, Aaron, and the children of Israel sang words that magnified Him. Moses' sister, Miriam, led the women to play timbrels, to sing and dance before the Lord. What a day of rejoicing! Exodus 15:20-21 paints a beautiful picture of this event. Miriam made a declaration of singing to the Lord for He had triumphed gloriously and caused Pharaoh's army to be thrown into the sea. She was a proud sister and a jubilant daughter of the Lord.

But not all that starts well ends well. With just a few ticks of the clock, singing turned into complaining. When Israelite bellies began to growl, their mouths followed suit. They informed Moses that remaining in Egypt would've been a better pay off in the long run. How quickly these freed slaves forgot what severe punishment they had endured under Pharaoh's harsh labor program: no day off and no straw for bricks! Did I mention the beatings?

But with desert heat beating down and no food in sight, accusations were flung like arrows. Take a look at Exodus 16:2-3(NIV): "In the desert the whole community grumbled against Moses and Aaron. The Israelites said to them, 'If only we had died by the LORD'S hand in Egypt. There we sat around pots of meat and ate all the food we wanted, but you have brought us out into this desert to starve this entire assembly to death.' "

Don't take the word *grumbled* lightly. It denotes *hostile complaining*, not merely whining. In my college years I served patrons at an upscale steak house. I learned the hard way that hungry people often are mean people. Entitlement brings out the worst in all of us.

It may seem as if the hungry Israelite grumblers were flying off the handle at Moses and Aaron; after all, they used the pronoun *you*. But in reality, the Israelites were complaining that *God* was not meeting *their demands*. Moses immediately gets this and refocuses the attention of the discontented mob. In verses 6-9 we read: "So Moses and Aaron said to all the Israelites, 'In the evening you will know that it was the LORD who brought you out of Egypt, and in the morning you will see the glory of the LORD, because he has heard your grumbling against him. Who are we that you should grumble against us?' Moses also said, 'You will know that it was the LORD when he gives you meat to eat in the evening and all the bread you want in the morning, because he has heard your grumbling against Him. Who are we? You are not grumbling against us, but against the LORD.' Then Moses told Aaron, 'Say to the entire community, 'Come before the LORD, for He has heard your complaints.' "

God provided manna and quail for the Israelites to eat. Hunger problem solved. The Israelites had full bellies; however, their complaining escalated. Why? Because grumbling is not a surface issues; it's deeper than that. Much deeper. The omniscient God, who created every one of these travelers, saw the depth of depravity in their hearts. Psalm 78:17-25 takes inventory: rebellion, testing, speaking against God, unbelief, and lack of trust.

When we hurl angry insults and complaints at others, there's a bitter root within acting like a catapult. Bitter root = bitter fruit. The Israelites should have dropped to their knees in prayer at the first pangs of hunger. Instead, they chose to pair stomach rumblings with verbal grumbling.

We've all been guilty of complaining—and here's what's a bit hard to swallow: A negative attitude is offensive to God. Period. In his book, *Lord, Change my Attitude*, James MacDonald says, "Those who choose murmuring as their lifestyle will spend their lifetimes in the wilderness."[iii] Ouch.

God doesn't bless grumbling. Why? Because the real target of such verbal trash is Him. Let's stop and think for a moment. We pray diligently for a spouse, a child, a job, a church, and a plethora of other things. And God answers our prayers. Then, lo and behold, one of those people, places, or things, inflicts pain on us. We begin to murmur about gifts we once cherished. The Gift Giver hears the grumbling. His name is the Lord Almighty. And He is not pleased.

I married one of the kindest men on the planet. He is gentle, loving, and more gracious than I deserve. He was my tall, dark, and handsome Ken doll. He believed I was his brunette Barbie. After the "I do's" had settled and real life started taking its toll, the dollhouse started to fall apart. I threw away my rose colored glasses and traded them in for a magnifying glass. Incidents I once brushed off as minor infractions had now escalated into big ordeals. My "grrr" sounds evolved from inward mumblings to outward grumblings. I complained to his face and then behind his back. The man I had prayed for and praised God for, was now a source of irritation. God had been so merciful to give me this man to have and to hold, not hold in contempt. I was no different than the Israelites. Fault finders are within God's radar. He hears and grieves when we mock His gifts. I've learned over the years to love my "Ken." He's not perfect, but I'm no Barbie either!

We live in a soured world, and God does allow unpleasant situations to enter our lives. He wants us to bring those things to Him. He desires to grow us into His likeness. Grumbling doesn't make us look one bit like our Heavenly Father, quite the contrary. Even if you were raised in a home of complainers, that doesn't mean it's inextricably bound to your DNA. With the strength of the Holy Spirit, you can shake it. I can shake it. It's a choice. If we choose constant grumbling and use others for verbal target practice, that's cesspool living. God takes offense when we offend others with our words because ultimately He is the real target.

Isaiah 40:27(NIV) asks, "Why do you complain, Jacob? Why do you say, Israel, 'My way is hidden from the LORD; my cause is disregarded by my God' "?

And James 5:9(NIV) tells us, "Don't grumble against one another, brothers and sisters or you will be judged. The Judge is standing at the door!" The story of the Israelites teaches us a vital lesson about word choice: God delights in the praises of His people; not the grumbling. He hears and He judges.

RIDICULOUS SPEAKING

I want to believe that had I seen the Red Sea part, bitter water turn sweet, and manna fall from I would not have doubted God as the Israelites did. The truth is I've had my own Red Sea partings. I've watched similar bread from heaven wind up on my kitchen table when I wasn't sure where the next meal was coming from. Yet, from time to time, I wonder if God sees my plight. I get impatient at His timing. Once, when my sky turned black with no sun in sight, I shook my fist at God. I can recall a few Christmas mornings when I felt slighted because I didn't open what I asked for. I pouted on Jesus' birthday, acting as if it was my day and not His. So, I can't judge the Israelite people whose faith grew dim while their ranting grew loud.

Impatience also is a catalyst for mouthing off. In Exodus 32:1-6, we learn that when Moses climbed the mountain to meet with God, the patience of the Israelites grew short—and their imaginations grew long. They brought to Aaron a really bad idea packaged in persuasive words. It seems they wanted a god with legs. Aaron bought into their short-sighted, God-eliminated scheme. Gold jewelry was thrown into a fire and presto; a golden calf popped out. Ok, that's not really how it happened. Aaron, intoxicated by persuasive words and perhaps intimidated by a pushy crowd, melted and molded gold (likely that given to the Israelites by the Egyptians) and formed a golden calf to be their new god to worship.

Impatience caused my first car accident. Fed up with the slow pokes in front of me, I whipped my car around a parking lot. Bam! I hit another vehicle. They too, had been impatient, and had taken matters into their own hands. We were both guilty of lacking good sense. While my father was grateful no bodily injuries occurred, he made me pay for the car's injury.

Aaron was originally appointed to be Moses' sidekick at the beginning of their journey because of his eloquence. It's sobering to see a man so gifted with words to be ultimately undone by them. In Exodus 32:21, Moses confronted Aaron: "What did these people do to you that you led them into such great sin?" Aaron wasn't quite so eloquent when faced with his sin. He backpedaled. He shifted the blame. He lied. "Do not be angry, my lord," Aaron answered. "You know how prone these people are to evil. They said to me, 'Make us gods who will go before us. As for this fellow Moses who brought us up out of Egypt, we don't know what has happened to him.' So I told them, 'Whoever has any gold jewelry, take it off.' Then they gave me the gold, and I threw it into the fire, and out came this calf!"

Seriously, a cow popped out of the fire? I know this was a devastating moment for Moses, but one has to wonder what his face looked like when he heard his brother's ridiculous words. That is what a lie is – ridiculous speaking.

Proverbs 12:19 (ESV) teaches us, "Truthful lips endure forever, but a lying tongue is but for a moment." When Moses asked Aaron about the golden calf, his older brother lied to his face! Aaron may have thought of the lie quickly, hoping it would be believed instantly, and forgotten rather quickly. But the lie went down in history. The eloquent and obedient brother will always be remembered for his preposterous story.

When we tell lies, we insult those we lie to. We treat them as if they're inferior in thinking and judgment. Moses judgment wasn't inferior, but he was infuriated. In Exodus 32:20, Moses took the golden calf "burned it in the fire, ground it to powder, scattered it on the water, and made the Israelites drink it." Hosea 10:13 speaks of eating the fruit of lies, but Aaron and the Israelites had to drink theirs. Pharaoh wasn't the only one who had to drink his sinful ways!

Scripture teaches much about lies and those who tell them. In Job 13:4, Job said that those who forge lies are like a physician of no value. (Ever paid for a doctor's visit only to find out he was clueless about your condition?) Those that delight in lies bless with their mouth, but curse inwardly. I once heard a woman say, "Love your hair," while she mumbled quietly, "Hate your guts."

WHITE LIES

Proverbs 14 exposes a false witness as one who has no problem telling lies. How often we hear the term "white lie." A white lie has a dark side somewhere, a bit of untruth. Who among us hasn't protected or pacified ourselves with a well-intentioned untruth? If we, like the fictional character Pinocchio, had our noses grow with our untruths, our words would be weighed with great caution.

Isaiah 28:15 describes a lie as a refuge and a falsehood which people hide themselves under. Joseph Goebbels said if you tell a lie big enough and keep repeating it, people will eventually come to believe it. I once knew a man whose life became one big lie. He told his lies so often; even he believed them to be true. This charming man conned everyone with his wit and wisdom, or so he thought. The day his character and lies were uncovered, he was left exposed. Attempting to get treasures by vanity and lies leaves a person tossed to and fro. Duplicity in speech spins a web of deceit. What we try to cover, God uncovers. What we uncover, God covers!

Some people dare to speak lies in the name of the Lord (Ezra 22:28; Jeremiah 29:23). This is forging God's signature on a check He didn't write. Today we call this "pulling out the God card." People use God as an excuse to enable their lies. "God told me to do this" or "God told me to say this." When my daughter was in college, I remember her telling me about a guy who dumped a girl by saying, "God told me not to marry you." Later, the girl discovered her boyfriend had several girlfriends.

When we tell lies, we love evil more than good (at least in the moment.) We sear our conscience when we continue in lies. We lead people astray and cause unbelievers to stumble. Aaron's lie as a leader was huge. He set a poor example in front of his people. He paid dearly for his lie. The Israelite people paid dearly for their sin of idol worship. The end of that day resulted in 3000 deaths.

The real truth? Lies grieve the heart of God.

GUILTY OF SLANDER

Earlier we read about Moses' sister, Miriam. She led the Israelite women in worship after the Red Sea crossing. As a young girl, she helped save the life of her baby brother Moses. She exhibited boldness in word and deed. When aligned with God's purposes, her strengths were assets.

Sadly, when we read Numbers 12, we find Miriam's bold words and deeds becoming weaknesses. Oswald Chambers warns of an unguarded strength being a double weakness. We must keep the strengths God has given us under submission. If not, our strengths can take us down for the count. Such was the case of Miriam as stated by Phineas Headley:

> "It is sad to turn from that jubilant procession led on by the fair prophetess to the scene of her fall. The Israelites reached the wilderness of Zin, and encamped on its extended plain. On each side stood the sentinel mountains, whose helmets of rock rent the folds of the summer cloud as it passed; the standards were unfurled, and the Tabernacle set up. Miriam had seen Moses robed in lightning on the smoking top of Sinai, and listened to the message from his lips when his brow shone like an angel's (Exodus 34:29-35). She had loved him as a part of her own being, since her lonely vigil by the river's side—but now ambition stalked through the chambers of her soul like a sceptered king, made the affections its vassals, and was environed by the train of riotous passions. Under the new

arrangement adopted by Moses at the suggestion of Jethro, his father-in-law (Exodus 18:13-24), the power was divided among captains, and her authority weakened. Besides, she had marked with jealousy the presence of Zipporah the Ethiopian in the camp, receiving the attention of the great leader, and the admiration of the multitude."[iv]

Perhaps Miriam's godly boldness had morphed into ungodly ambition. Or maybe pride had taken up residence in Miriam's heart. The mouth speaks from the overflow of the heart, and what Miriam chose to say about her brother Moses wasn't pretty: "Miriam and Aaron began to talk against Moses because of his Cushite wife, for the had married a Cushite. 'Has he Lord spoken only through Moses?' they asked. 'Hasn't he also spoken through us?'" And the Lord heard this." Numbers 12:1-2(NIV)

Whatever heart problem she had, Miriam failed to bring it to the Lord for healing or correction. Once again, we have a case of inner bitterness being vomited onto another individual. Miriam cast her angry thoughts about Moses onto Aaron. These dueling banjos weren't making a joyful noise. The omnipresent God of the universe heard the sibling slander. The result was Miriam being stricken with leprosy and set outside the camp for seven days, a living example of the toxic effects of unclean speech.

We see from this incident that God abhors slanderous speech. Leviticus 19:16(NIV) reads, "Do not go about spreading slander among your people. Do not do anything that endangers your neighbor's life. I am the LORD." The book of Proverbs reminds us that it is foolish to slander. The mudslinger winds up knee deep in mud! Slander separates friends and families. The seven days Miriam spent outside the camp separated from everyone she loved must have felt like an eternity. She certainly had time to think about word choices. God was Moses' greatest defender in this incident. His thoughts and words about Moses trumped anything Miriam or Aaron thought or said. (It's interesting to note that although Aaron didn't squelch his sister's rantings, Miriam was held most responsible, perhaps because she incited the private riot.)

I'm thankful the Lord has withheld leprosy from me when I've spoken against others. Just reading the account again makes me want to keep my mouth zipped. When my opinions could hurt another person, they need to be left at the feet of Jesus and not dumped in someone's ears.

FINISHING SHORT OF THE GOAL

Moses was a man whom God loved. Exodus 33:11 tells us God spoke to Moses face to face as one speaks to a friend. God's relationship with Moses was clearly remarkable. God loved this imperfect man! Though He knew Moses would make an error that would bring great grief upon himself and some of his people, God used Moses anyway. That gives me hope.

In Numbers 12, we learn Moses erred big time. God gave Moses a command to carry out in front of the Israelites. His plan was for Moses to speak to a rock, and God would make water flow from it. Instead, Moses spoke to the Israelites with angry words and hit the rock twice. Sure, the people and the animals drank, but no one marveled. I wonder if they ever even acknowledged the miracle of the water gushing from the rock. There's no mention of any marveling. The Israelites just lapped up the H_2O and never said thank you to Moses or sang praises to God. Perhaps they were afraid of the wrath that spewed out of Moses, even as the water flowed from the rock.

The consequences of Moses' action were devastating. Moses was not able to deliver into the Promised Land the people he loved. As a leader, he had roared when just a simple sentence would've taken care of business. Because he disobeyed God, Moses only got to see the land of promise from afar. He never put his feet across the finish line in a race he had worked so hard for so many years to win.

A leader is to live above reproach. James 3:1 speaks of a teacher being judged more strictly than others. Moses was the teacher of the Israelites. Although God's love for him never changed, His judgment on Moses was a demonstration to the Israelites about the importance of honoring and revering the Lord God as holy. Moses was God's representative to the people. God was going to be gracious and give the water out of His goodness and longsuffering. In a moment when his words and actions should have displayed the attributes of God, Moses showed the ugly side of flesh. David Guzik comments:

> "Worst of all, Moses defaced a beautiful picture of Jesus' redemptive work through the rock which provided water in the wilderness. The New Testament makes it clear this water-providing, life-giving rock was a picture of Jesus (1 Corinthians 10:4). Jesus, being struck once, provided life for all who

would drink of Him (John 7:37). But was unnecessary - and unrighteous - that Jesus would be struck again, much less again twice, because the Son of God needed only to suffer once (Hebrews 10:10-12). Jesus can now be come to with words of faith (Romans 10:8-10), as Moses should have only used words of faith to bring life-giving water to the nation of Israel. Moses 'ruined' this picture of the work of Jesus God intended."[v]

Guzik goes on to say, "At the end of it all, God *was* seen as holy among the children of Israel. Moses did not hallow God in this incident, but God hallowed Himself through the correction of Moses. God will get His glory; God will be hallowed, but will it come through our obedience or our correction?"[vi]

We shake our heads in pity for Moses. His job was tough. We can sympathize with his behavior. However, God needed to correct this leader. Various research indicates that only one out of three biblical leaders finishes well.

As for the Israelites, the water they drank that day was called the water of Meribah, which means *strife, contention, or quarreling*. Moses' band of followers will be linked throughout history with these derogatory descriptors.

We are remembered for our words and deeds. Speak wisely. Act wisely. Finish well!

MOMENTS IN THE MIRROR

CHAPTER 2

1. The Israelites groaned, moaned and grumbled. Are you guilty of the same behavior?

2. What were you grumbling about? To whom did you grumble? Who heard you? Who overheard you?

3. Does grumbling really achieve anything?

4. Name a time you told a lie to get away with something. Who were you actually lying to?

5. Have you ever hurt someone's reputation by speaking ill of them to another individual? If you have done this, explain why.

6. Could you ever be perceived as a slanderer?

7. Even the great leader Moses spoke out of anger and hurt himself and others. Have you ever been guilty of this?

8. Have angry words or actions caused your life to be altered in any way?

"FILL HER UP!"

Intimacy with God equips us for socializing outside our "holy of holies" places.

When I was a child, my dad would pull up to a gas station and tell the attendant to "Fill her up." The tank would get filled while my dad and I sat in the car. The attendant would also clean the windshield and check under the hood —for no extra charge! These days, I fill my own gas tank. I decide what fuel grade I want to put in my car and how much of it I want.

I also make those choices for my mouth. I choose who will fill my mouth with words. I choose what kind of words I want to run from my mouth. And these choices make a huge difference in my life and the lives of others.

FAMOUS LAST WORDS

Before Moses' death, he gathered his people together and reviewed all the things God had done for them. He repeated the words God had spoken throughout their journey to the Promised Land. This faithful servant reminded the people of Israel about past mistakes, which would serve as a reminder of how to approach the future. To ensure a safe and prosperous journey, Moses exhorted them to follow God and to remember all the words He had used to fill their tanks. God had spoken words into the ears of Moses. Moses then filled the tanks of his people with those words.

Moses vividly recalled when he chose to speak his own words rather than God's. It caused a major breakdown, one more costly than Moses ever imagined. I believe this faithful leader didn't want anyone to repeat his error. Let's read his words in Deuteronomy 30:11-14 (ESV):

> "For this commandment that I command you today is not too hard for you, neither is it far off. It is not in heaven, that you should say, 'Who will ascend to heaven for us and bring it to us that we may hear it and do it?' Neither is it beyond the sea, that you should say, 'Who will go over the sea for us and bring it to us that we may hear it and do it?' But the word is very near you. It is in your mouth and in your heart, so that you can do it."

What Moses was communicating is actually quite simple and so applicable to us today: If the pure words of God are in our hearts and in our mouths, we can successfully travel the distance through life. If God fills our tanks, we won't run out of fuel. Our engines won't corrode, and we won't spew smog in the air that others will be forced to inhale.

God's pure words are found in the Bible, which serves as a filter for our own words. It's a filter we must access every day. Philippians 4:8 exhorts us to think on what is true, honest, just pure, lovely, of good report, and virtuous. If we adhered to these adjectives in filtering our words, we might pass the clean air conversation test.

I once fell prey to an obscene phone caller. The man informed me he was conducting a survey for a well-known clothing manufacturer. He then proceeded to ask me a series of questions about his company's products. Since I was fixing lunch for my five year old, and could multitask, I decided to be courteous and show favor on this unsuspecting telemarketer. Because the clothing items were of personal nature, the questions were as well. Initially, I convinced myself the questions were uncomfortable but they did correlate with the product. At last I realized I was divulging information to a pervert! I let the man have it with no filter in place. Then I violently slammed the phone down. My daughter looked at me with tears in her eyes. She had never heard her mommy utter such verbiage before. I was embarrassed to have spoken with such cruelty. Apologies were in order for my naïve little girl. Emotions justified my actions, but my words still needed to be filtered.

Automobiles are required to pass emissions testing annually; our mouths need to pass edification testing constantly. Our cars require regular maintenance to keep them in good running order. Our mouths are no different. If an engine stalls or will barely crank, something is wrong with the car. Can you see the correlation with the mouth? We can check manuals to identify problems with our cars. We can check God's Word to identify problems with our mouths. The Holy Spirit is the attendant who can tell us what's wrong — what needs fixing and why.

PROPHETIC WORDS

Joshua 1:8 (ESV) clearly reveals the vital connection between the mouth and the Word of God:

> "This Book of the Law shall not depart from your mouth, but you shall meditate on it day and night, so that you may be careful to do according to all that is written in it. For then you will make your way prosperous, and then you will have good success."

Throughout the Old Testament, we see examples of God filling prophets with His life-changing words. When the prophet Isaiah stood before the Israelites, he needed God to fill his mouth with the words to speak. In Isaiah 51:16, God told the Israelites through Isaiah that He, Jehovah, had put His words in their mouths.

In Jeremiah 1:9-10, we learn that God put words in Jeremiah's mouth to accomplish incredible things: He would be able to rule over nations and kingdoms, to root out and pull down, to destroy and throw down, to build and to plant. Sure, talk can be cheap, but Jeremiah quickly learned that words in action can accomplish much. God said He would make His words fire in Jeremiah's mouth and the people as wood. Fire-breathing is God's job, never ours. If we ever become fire-breathing dragons and God didn't ignite the fire, we'd better be wearing flame-retardant garments; otherwise, we'll be burned by our own words. When Jeremiah was filled with God's words (Scripture tell us he said he ate them), he felt joyful. Rejoicing can keep us going, even through the roughest terrains.

God also told Ezekiel He would open the prophet's mouth and put in what was to be spoken. Whoever would not receive what the Lord poured through Ezekiel would be considered rebellious (Ezekiel 3:27). In the same way, God pours His words of wisdom through the wise people He places around us. Wise people are the nozzles God uses to pump his fuel. And it's okay to guzzle! In Psalm 119:131, David stated he opened his mouth and "panted," longing for God's commandments.

MENTORS

I've had mentors in my life who poured God's Word into my needy tank. When I didn't know where to look for wisdom, they led me to the true source — the Bible. They knew the words of God I had forgotten (or had never even heard) would make a world of difference. I was able to get back in the race because of wise people speaking into my life.

The Lord gifted me with a friend and mentor, Dianne. She is a wise woman who speaks with power and conviction. When the Lord started impressing on my heart His desire for me to speak, teach, and write, I called Dianne. I recited all the reasons the notion was ridiculous. She patiently listened and then shocked me with words of wisdom, "Dawn, God made you with these gifts. Now why are you going to tell Him no? Are you going to mock the hand the hand of God who made you?" I surrendered my life and gifts to my maker because my mentor challenged my excuses.

Wise counselors will always direct to the Word of God. They will remind us not to depart from the commandment of His lips, to treasure the words of His mouth more than necessary food (Job 23:12 NKJV). If my mentors had watered down the truths of Scripture to make me feel better, I may have stayed on the sidelines, licking the lashes of other's harsh words—or withdrawing from the journey altogether. A solution of half water/half gasoline will stop a car altogether. When watered down, the words of God can be ineffective as well.

In Malachi 2:6, the priests of Levi were to have the law of truth in their mouths. They were not to mix the law with injustice. We need to ensure we do not corrupt God's Word by aligning it with any bitterness or self-righteousness. We are not to add to or diminish the words of the Lord. His words, as described in Psalm 12:6 (NKJV), are as "pure as silver tried in a furnace of earth and purified seven times."

I have a friend whose father was a preacher. He would use the pulpit to take a verse of Scripture and beat his family up with it. His motive was to humiliate them into obedience, not to teach the Word of God to an entire flock. He would misuse what God intended for correction, and use it to abuse, punish, and humiliate. God never intended His Word for maligned purposes.

Contrast this preacher's approach with the example set by Jesus. When Jesus opened His mouth, He taught. Those who heard Him marveled at the gracious words that proceeded from His mouth. In Luke 21:15, the Son of God told the disciples He would give them a mouth of wisdom. Running low on good advice? Seek the Son. He dispenses the highest-grade fuel to run on.

OPENED AND CLOSED CASES

Throughout Scripture, God reminds us that He made the mouth. He will teach us what to say, how to answer, and when to speak. He opens the mouth; He closes the mouth.

In Luke 1, the angel Gabriel appeared to an elderly priest named Zacharias as he was ministering in the temple. The angel told Zacharias his wife Elizabeth would bear a son whom he was to name John. The aged man doubted the words of Gabriel and asked for a sign. Zacharias wanted to know the words the angel of God uttered would come to pass. Zacharias' unbelief led to his silencing. We must continually pray that unbelief doesn't cloud our hearts, leaving us doubting and quieted when God desires so much more for us!

The "when to speak" issue is critical throughout Scripture — and its critical today. Timing is everything. Ask the runner who loses by a fraction of a second, the business person whose delay in traffic causes a missed flight, or the ER doctor who states that extra minutes would have saved the life of a loved one. Timing matters!

Let's take a look at the life of Abigail, whose story begins in 1 Samuel 25. She's the beautiful wife of Nabal, a man with an ugly attitude. His name means *fool* — and his actions followed suit.

When David was on the run from Saul, he camped out near the property of Nabal, who owned much land and livestock. As long as David and his army were camped out by Nabal's property, no animal thefts took place. Animal thievery was commonplace in that day.

At some point, David and his men grew hungry, and sent a messenger to ask Nabal for food and provisions since their encampment had prospered the man. Nabal balked at what he thought was an absurd request. He declined these men any recompense for how he had prospered by David's temporary residence.

Nabal's servants knew this foolish response could result in an attack on his household. One of the servants ran to Abigail and told her the dilemma. To save her home and her servants, this God-fearing woman took action. In 1 Samuel 25:19, we learn that Abigail made a plan but did not tell Nabal. To confront her husband would have escalated the impending disaster. Abigail was wise to hold her tongue. She followed the wisdom of Proverbs 23:9 (ESV) that clearly warns "Do not speak in the hearing of a fool, for he will despise the good sense of your words."

Abigail brought David and his men provisions and also gave wise counsel. Her demeanor and her words saved David from acting foolishly. He respected the way Abigail spoke and the wisdom in her words. Here's his response found in 1 Samuel 25:32-35 (NKJV):

> "And David said to Abigail, 'Blessed be the LORD, the God of Israel, who sent you this day to meet me! Blessed be your discretion, and blessed be you, who have kept me this day from bloodguilt and from working salvation with my own hand! For as surely as the LORD, the God of Israel, lives, who has restrained me from

hurting you, unless you had hurried and come to meet me, truly by morning there had not been left to Nabal so much as one male.' Then David received from her hand what she had brought him. And he said to her, 'Go up in peace to your house. See, I have obeyed your voice, and I have granted your petition.'"

When Abigail returned home, she found her husband drunk. Once again, she knew the timing was everything and withheld her words. Verse 26 reads, "...she told him nothing, little or much, until morning light." Ecclesiastes 3:7 reveals there is a time to keep silence and a time to speak. This story ends with Nabal's death and David's proposal of marriage to Abigail.

A wise person knows what words to say, how to say them, and when to say them. Proverbs 25:11 makes the importance of word choice clear: "Like apples of gold in settings of silver is a word spoken in right circumstances" (NASB). Abigail took the gold in all three categories.

Consider these additional verses that speak to value of verbal discretion.

"The Lord GOD has given me the tongue of the learned, that I should know how to speak a word in season to him that is weary: he awakens morning by morning, he awakens my ear to hear as the learned" Isaiah 50:4 (KJV).

"Teach me and I will hold my tongue" Job 6:24 (NKJV).

"...let every person be quick to hear, slow to speak, slow to anger" James 1:19 (ESV).

"Keep silence before me, O coastlands; and let the people renew their strength: let them come near; **then** let them speak..." Isaiah 41:1 (KJV).

I bolded the word *then* in Isaiah 41:1 to emphasize that the children of Israel received God's strength only when they first came near to Him and listened to Him. When we draw near to God, He draws near to us. Only when we have spent time with Him and have learned His words are we capable of speaking. Listening to Him and *then* speaking is always the proper order.

There have been many times in my life when people have come to me for advice. How incredible it is to have just spent time in God's Word on the very subject they have broached me about. We learn in 1 Peter 3:15 to "honor Christ the Lord as holy, always being prepared to make a defense to anyone who asks you for a reason for the hope that is in you...." When we're in the habit of honoring Christ as holy, people will be curious. We're better prepared to be lighthouses for those needing direction. Intimacy with God equips us for socializing outside our "holy of holies" places.

Neglecting intimacy with God and dwelling on circumstances can lead to anxiety. Abigail and her household would've gone up in smoke if she'd held a pity party. But she didn't focus on her frailty as a woman or the fury she must have felt toward Nabal. Either would've blinded her eyes — and possibly lit her tongue. Instead, Abigail calmly focused on the mighty power of God. Trust — plus action and well-chosen words — led to the fall of Nabal and victory for the righteous

As we close this chapter, here are two powerful mouth guard verses to commit to memory:

"The heart of the wise teaches his mouth and adds learning to his lips" (Proverbs 16:23 KJV).

"The heart of the righteous studieth to answer" (Prov. 15:28a)

MOMENTS IN THE MIRROR

CHAPTER 3

1. How often do you fill up your mouth tank? Where do you go for the filling?

2. When was the last time you "panted" to be filled with the Word of God?

3. Do you think before you speak to filter your words? Are you guilty of speaking first and not filtering your words?

4. Would you say you are most likely to be quick to speak or slow to speak?

5. Do you identify more with Abigail or her husband Nabal?

6. How are you doing in the "what to say, how to say it, and when to say it" categories? List areas in which you may need improvement.

7. Are you more likely to dispense common-sense solutions to others or truth from the Word of God?

8. Would you ever water down God's Word to make someone feel better about a situation?

SAFE EXITS

The words we speak have the power to disintegrate or elevate our reputations.

I have a friend with a strange quirk. Don't chuckle. We all have peculiarities. None of us is normal. Author and speaker Patsy Clairmont says, "*Normal* is just a setting on your dryer." Anyway, my friend's quirk is scoping out fire exits when she enters a building. She frequently travels with her husband on business trips. Upon entering a hotel, she asks about the locations of the fire exits. When she arrives in her room, she immediately looks on the back of the door, where the fire escapes are mapped out and posted for safety measures. She also scopes out restaurants, movie theaters, and any place there's a possibility of getting trapped. The first time I heard her confess this quirk, I shook my head in wonder. I had never given a second thought to scoping out emergency doors. I entered and exited buildings without a second thought

THINKING BEFORE SPEAKING

My friend's perpetual quest for safe exits has generated lots of second thoughts about my words. Too often I speak without thinking about what's exiting my mouth. Ever heard of "open mouth, insert foot" syndrome? I've suffered from this malady far too many times. I've been guilty of flippantly spouting careless remarks, and I've wounded others in the process. I've embarrassed loved ones by joking about their mistakes, causing them to head for the nearest exits. Although I didn't intend to hurt or humiliate others, I did. The repercussions later caused me great pain. If I had taken the time to guard my mouth, my reputation would have remained intact, and others would have avoided pain, which is even more important.

The words we speak have the power to disintegrate or elevate our reputations. Winston Churchill, who had strong verbal skills, once said, "We are masters of the unsaid words, but slaves of those we let slip out." Compare the impact of his insulting quote "I may be drunk, Miss, but in the morning, I will be sober, and you will still be ugly" to the invigorating "Never, never, never give up." The first quote, spoken when Churchill was not in total control of his faculties or his tongue, has made many people laugh, but it likely wounded an individual for life. The latter quote, spoken with calmness and verve, continues to inspire people to greatness even today. Both quotes exited the same mouth — but with decidedly different results.

JEZEBEL'S WORDS

The life of Jezebel is quite a story about the consequences of words. In 1 Kings 16:30, the marriage of Jezebel and King Ahab begins. Ahab had done more to provoke the Lord than all the kings of Israel before him. Unfortunately, this husband and wife were evenly matched in terms of wickedness. Jezebel actually murdered the prophets of the Lord (1 Kings 18:4). God sent His prophet Elijah to demonstrate the power of God before this devious couple. With that power, Elijah killed 450 prophets of Baal — Jezebel's former dinner guests.

To say she was furious with Elijah would be a gross understatement. (I once saw "Jezebel Sauce" at a grocery store. I didn't even think about purchasing it because I knew it would be hard to swallow!) When Ahab told Jezebel about the deaths, she sent these hot words to Elijah: "So may the gods do to me and more also, if I do not make your life as the life of one of them by this time tomorrow." (1 Kings 19:2 ESV) With cruel confidence and smoking words, Jezebel taunted her adversary Elijah.

In 1 Kings 19:1, Ahab recounted to Jezebel all the miracles performed by God through Elijah on Mount Carmel. God sent fire from heaven and rain after years of drought. But the God of Elijah and the miracles He sent through His prophet, didn't faze this haughty woman. She believed herself to be more powerful than Elijah and his God. Evil pumped through her heart and veins — and spilled out of her mouth. Jezebel thought way too highly of herself. She exalted herself by assertion of authority over her husband, over the prophet of God, and over other men in the land. She flattered herself in opinion, action, and speech. This proved to be a deadly stance.

Proverbs 16:18 (NIV) explains, "Pride goes before destruction, and a haughty spirit before a fall." And Jezebel had quite a fall. Her last taunting words, spoken to Jehu, the new king over Israel, were filled with venom and sarcasm. Those words and the words she had hurled at Elijah years before were costly. She was thrown from a window, trampled by a horse, and eaten by dogs. Only her skull, feet, and hands remained when the carnage ended. (2 Kings 9:30-37). It was a long, ugly fall for a woman who thought so highly of herself!

DON'T FLATTER YOURSELF

I receive a daily devotional from Boyd Bailey entitled *Wisdom Hunters.*

Here's part of his devotional on self-flattery.

> "Self-flattery is foolish. It has no fear of God. Self-flattery follows a false faith that is forged out of convenience, not commitment. Self-flattery sees itself as the center of attention instead of Almighty God. It is enamored with itself. It defines and executes its own agenda. It is soft on sin. However, God-fearers see their sin and flee from its presence. It is not invited into their circle of influence. Furthermore, a person who flatters himself has neither a proper view of God nor any respect for Him. Respect for God flows from fear of God, but self-flattery demands respect. They need to know that others hold the same high opinion of themselves as they do.
>
> Self-flattery heaps praise on itself in substitute for penance. This is dangerously absurd. Even the silliest bird does not set a trap for itself. Smoothing over our conduct or soothing our conscience may set us up for failure. We can justify anything, but we had better be ready to suffer the consequences. There is a limit to our self-congratulation. Eventually, God and others grow impatient with our obnoxious ways. Our inability to own up to our actions — or lack thereof — lowers our standing with God and man. Self-flattery is a losing proposition. It loses respect instead of gaining respect. It grows discontent instead of being content. It feels worse instead of feeling better. Self-flattery fails. There are many forms of self-flattery. When we think we are smarter than God, ignoring the principles laid out in His word, we flatter ourselves. When we think we have hope in heaven, but we act like hell, we flatter ourselves. When we live for today as if death were a million miles away, we flatter ourselves. When we treat others with contempt, then expect them to follow our ways, we flatter ourselves. When we say we trust in the Lord, but borrow money and presume on the future, we flatter ourselves. Self-flattery longs for approval, but it is denied from those who really matter. There is a better way. The better way rises above self-flattery's deception."[vii]

Jezebel didn't rise above self-flattery. She fell under it. Figuratively and literally!

Psalm 12:3-4 (NKJV) tells us:

"May the Lord cut off all flattering lips, And the tongue that speaks proud things, Who have said, 'With our tongue we will prevail; Our lips are our own; Who is lord over us?' "

The Bible warns against thinking highly of ourselves. Jezebel's demise is a stern visual for the boaster who leaves God out of the equation.

People who brag or boast in self are subject to falling off their cheap and flimsy pedestals. Our works, our lives, and our fruit-bearing should be our witness — and what propels others to speak highly of us. "Let another praise you, and not your own mouth; a stranger, and not your own lips" (Proverbs 27:2 ESV).

To boast of anything other than the Lord or His great works is to bring glory to self. "My soul makes its boast in the LORD; let the humble hear and be glad" (Psalm 34:2 ESV). The Bible warns of even boasting in tomorrow's plans. None of us knows what the end of each day may bring. God is in control and may change circumstances in a heartbeat. My pastor always prefaces his plans with the phrase, "Lord willing." What we desire to happen may not be the Lord's will, and boasting is foolish. I'm not saying there is anything wrong with vision casting or sharing hopes and dreams, but to hold tightly to those plans (and even brag about them) is a set-up for a fall.

Have you ever been around a boaster? Pretty nauseating isn't it? A boaster keeps "me, myself, and I" as the main topics of conversation. A boaster fails to include others while conversing.

My husband and I love to entertain guests. We try to invite friends and acquaintances over almost weekly. We love to share meals and life with other folks. There have been times, however, when guests have bid *adieu*, and I was left feeling insignificant. They had boasted and bragged and never once asked my husband and me anything about us.

I must admit, I've been guilty of monopolizing conversations too. I'm a talker. I come from a long line of talkers. My mother used to say I came out of the womb talking. I've often prided myself as being the one to keep conversations going. But as I've matured, I now see the value in the phrase, "Silence is golden." Silence often allows the quiet person time to gain enough confidence to add something golden to a conversation. Silence can be more powerful than words. There is a time to speak and a time to be silent.

IDLE CHATTER

Idle chatter is also a fruitless exiting of words. Proverbs 14:23 (NKJV) reads, "In all labor there is profit, but idle chatter leads only to poverty." If I had a nickel for every useless phone conversation I've been party to, I'd be a rich woman by now. Idle chatter is a waste of time.

"Idle hands are the devil's workshop," isn't a quote from the Bible, but it illustrates biblical truth found in 2 Thessalonians 3:11 and 1 Timothy 5:13. And it certainly applies to the women of Sodom: "Behold, this was the iniquity of thy sister Sodom, pride, fullness of bread, and abundance of idleness was in her and in her daughters, neither did she strengthen the hand of the poor and needy." (Ezekiel 16:49 NKJV).

The women of Sodom wasted their days. They had no compassion or time to spare for those less fortunate than themselves. Can't you just picture those women eating and chatting, eating and chatting, eating and chatting?

Women often get a bad rap for being talkative. Often times we deserve it. Some of us use our allotted words for the day in destructive or just plain useless ways. How sad the women of Sodom didn't use their abundance of wealth and time to serve those in need. They chose to live with no regard for others. You and I can go to the fields of our communities in times of abundance to honor God and others. We can be kingdom builders any place, any time. Going to the throne more than the phone is a safe plan to keep our mouths from danger.

GOSSIP DRAGONS

Engaging in gossip is like running from a burning building with fire ablaze on the tongue. Everyone gets burned: the one with the flaming tongue, the one listening to the sizzle, and the one who is the subject of the fire. Like fire-breathing dragons, some wait for opportune moments to breathe hot, venomous gossip to destroy another person's destiny or testimony. James 3:6 (ESV) tells us, "And the tongue is a fire, a world of unrighteousness. The tongue is set among our members, staining the whole body, setting on fire the entire course of life, and set on fire by hell."

Fire doesn't burn only in hell or in fireplaces. Fire can light the tongue with words that can burn people, relationships, families, and churches. Fire is best when kept within the fireplace. When fire ventures out where it shouldn't – we must beware! Proverbs 16:27 (KJV) warns us, "An ungodly man digs up evil, and it is on his lips like burning fire."

After surrendering to Christ, I immersed myself in the pages from Genesis to Revelation. I was both humbled and awed by the words of Scripture. Hebrews 4:12 (NIV) states, "For the word of God is alive and active. Sharper than any double-edged sword, it penetrates even to dividing soul and spirit, joints and marrow; it judges the thoughts and attitudes of the heart." I ached with desire to teach these sparkling gems from the Old and New Testament to anyone who would listen. So I enrolled as a Bible study teacher at my church. One day after class, a woman complimented me as a gifted and passionate teacher. I was just about to blush with excitement. Then she stated she'd hesitated to sign up for my class in the beginning. A woman had been spreading gossip that I was a terrible teacher. I did blush then. How humiliating to hear those words. My face felt like it was on fire. I had to deal with the fire in my heart on the way home that day.

The words that exit our mouths must honor God, us, and others. We are responsible for making godly exit choices. And the exit instructions for word selection are found, not behind a door but between the bindings of the Bible.

CHAPTER 4

1. How would others describe the words that exit your mouth?

2. Do you thoughtfully consider what you will say before you speak?

3. Flattery is not beneficial to the one giving or the one receiving such speech. Can you think of a time when you flattered someone? If so, what were your motives?

4. Has anyone ever tried to flatter (not give a sincere compliment) you? If so, what was your reaction?

5. How do you handle a boaster?

6. Are you ever guilty of boasting? If so, what do you boast about and why?

7. Would you describe yourself as one who can chatter for hours? How much time would you say you waste weekly in idle chatter?

8. Do you set fires with your tongue?

9. What aspect of this chapter resonated most with you?

TRUTH OR CONSEQUENCES

In a crumbling society, people will listen to anyone who offers hope,

even if it is a false one.

There's a city in southern New Mexico actually named Truth or Consequences. Such an odd name for a place to live! If you twist the truth in that city, do you reap consequences? The name leaves one to speculate if a dishonest person would dare move there.

Husband and wife duo Ananias and Sapphira landed in a real life truth-or-consequences dilemma, one they crafted because deceit reigned in their hearts. Their story takes place in the beginning days of the church. Believers were said to be of one heart and one soul. No one lacked, for all sold their property and houses. They gave their earnings to the apostles to be distributed. The banners of generosity and grace waved over the people. Here's the story of Ananias and his wife, as told in Acts 5:1-11(ESV):

> "But a man named Ananias, with his wife Sapphira, sold a piece of property, and with his wife's knowledge he kept back for himself some of the proceeds and brought only a part of it and laid it at the apostles' feet. But Peter said, 'Ananias, why has Satan filled your heart to lie to the Holy Spirit and to keep back for yourself part of the proceeds of the land? While it remained unsold, did it not remain your own? And after it was sold, was it not at your disposal? Why is it that you have contrived this deed in your heart? You have not lied to men but to God.' When Ananias heard these words, he fell down and breathed his last. And great fear came upon all who heard of it. The young men rose and wrapped him up and carried him out and buried him. After an interval of about three hours his wife came in, not knowing what had happened. And Peter said to her, 'Tell me whether you sold the land for so much.' And she said, 'Yes, for so much.' But Peter said to her, 'How is it that you have agreed together to test the Spirit of the Lord? Behold, the feet of those who have buried your husband are at the door, and they will carry you out.' Immediately she fell down at his feet and breathed her

the land.

The words of individuals can impact lives, but often the power of words increases with number of people joining them. A majority opinion can rule even when it's wrong. Here's an example.

The children of Israel were God's chosen people. In Genesis Chapter 12 the Lord spoke to Abraham. He was commanded to leave his country and family and begin a journey filled with promises. As the plan unfolded, the Israelites were to move in a destination of God's choosing –the Promised Land, under the leadership of Abraham and later to Moses. It's a long story, but a trip that should've taken a few days stretched into a laborious 40-year trek (Deuteronomy 1:2-3). Abraham died along the way.

What caused all the detours and mishaps along the way? Morale was low, fear was high, and negative words were abundant — a combination that spells trouble. Chapters 13 and 14 of the book of Numbers highlight the story of Moses, Abraham's successor, and one leg of the Promised Land trip that was held up by the negative words of a fearful majority.

In Numbers 13:1, the Lord speaks to Moses and tells him to send spies into the land of Canaan (the Promised Land). Twelve spies were sent out to take inventory of the land. They were to inspect the fruitfulness of the land, the attitude of its people, and the strength of its army.

Moses instructed the spies to approach their mission courageously (Numbers 13:20). But only two of the twelve spies, Joshua and Caleb, followed his instruction. What the spies saw in Canaan was jaw dropping. The fruit of the land was abundant. What about the men of the land? Well, they were abundant too — and huge. Ten of the spies returned to Moses drenched in fear. When Moses inquired about the status of the land, the majority agreed the land was flowing with milk and honey — but the size of the men made taking the land impossible. Here are the words of the majority of the spies found in Numbers 13:31-33 (ESV):

> "31 But the men who had gone up with him said, 'We are not able to go up against the people, for they are stronger than we.' 32 And they gave the children of Israel a bad report of the land which they had spied out, saying, "The land through which we have gone as spies is a land that devours its inhabitants, and all the people whom we saw in it are men of great stature. 33 There we saw the giant (the descendants of Anak came from the giants);

last. When the young men came in they found her dead, and they carried her out and buried her beside her husband. And great fear came upon the whole church and upon all who heard of these things."

Remember the consequences of Aaron's lie and the Israelite's problem with telling the truth? Well, there's more to discuss about mouths that speak the truth and mouths that twist the truth. We call them fibs, jokes, exaggerations, and a host of other subtleties. The truth is, they're words that don't represent the truth at all.

Proverbs 6:16-19 lists seven things the Lord hates. A lying tongue is listed right beside hands that shed innocent blood. That's sobering!

The book of Proverbs has much to say about the problem of verbal inaccuracy. Slowly read the following verses from Proverbs 11 (ESV). Highlight anything that has to do with truth versus dishonesty.

> 1 A false balance is an abomination to the LORD,
>   but a just weight is his delight.
> 2 When pride comes, then comes disgrace,
>   but with the humble is wisdom.
> 3 The integrity of the upright guides them,
>   but the crookedness of the treacherous destroys them.
> 4 Riches do not profit in the day of wrath,
>   but righteousness delivers from death.
> 5 The righteousness of the blameless keeps his way straight,
>   but the wicked falls by his own wickedness.
> 6 The righteousness of the upright delivers them,
>   but the treacherous are taken captive by their lust.
> 7 When the wicked dies, his hope will perish,
>   and the expectation of wealth[a] perishes too.
> 8 The righteous is delivered from trouble,
>   and the wicked walks into it instead.
> 9 With his mouth the godless man would destroy his neighbor,
>   but by knowledge the righteous are delivered.
> 10 When it goes well with the righteous, the city rejoices,
>   and when the wicked perish there are shouts of gladness.
> 11 By the blessing of the upright a city is exalted,
>   but by the mouth of the wicked it is overthrown.
> 12 Whoever belittles his neighbor lacks sense,
>   but a man of understanding remains silent.
> 13 Whoever goes about slandering reveals secrets,

but he who is trustworthy in spirit keeps a thing covered.
14 Where there is no guidance, a people falls,
    but in an abundance of counselors there is safety.
15 Whoever puts up security for a stranger will surely suffer harm,
    but he who hates striking hands in pledge is secure.
16 A gracious woman gets honor,
    and violent men get riches.
17 A man who is kind benefits himself,
    but a cruel man hurts himself.
18 The wicked earns deceptive wages,
    but one who sows righteousness gets a sure reward.
19 Whoever is steadfast in righteousness will live,
    but he who pursues evil will die.
20 Those of crooked heart are an abomination to the LORD,
    but those of blameless ways are his delight.
21 Be assured, an evil person will not go unpunished,
    but the offspring of the righteous will be delivered.
22 Like a gold ring in a pig's snout
    is a beautiful woman without discretion.
23 The desire of the righteous ends only in good;
    the expectation of the wicked in wrath.
24 One gives freely, yet grows all the richer;
    another withholds what he should give, and only suffers want.
25 Whoever brings blessing will be enriched,
    and one who waters will himself be watered.
26 The people curse him who holds back grain,
    but a blessing is on the head of him who sells it.
27 Whoever diligently seeks good seeks favor,
    but evil comes to him who searches for it.
28 Whoever trusts in his riches will fall,
    but the righteous will flourish like a green leaf.
29 Whoever troubles his own household will inherit the wind, and the fool will be servant to the wise of heart.
30 The fruit of the righteous is a tree of life,
    and whoever captures souls is wise.
31 If the righteous is repaid on earth,
    how much more the wicked and the sinner!

Too bad Ananias and Sapphira didn't have Proverbs 11 memorized as words to live by. Their dishonest scales didn't tip favorably before the Lord.

Years ago, I gave the clerk at the Department of Motor Vehicles (DMV) my desired weight, not my actual weight. I was on a diet and getting close to my goal. I was just a few pounds off the weight I quoted for my license. Never the less, the poundage I gave him was a lie. Convincing myself the inaccuracy would soon become accurate, I tipped the scales in my favor but not God's. I'd laid aside the fact God hates dishonest scales. You'd better believe I stuck to my diet to ensure that my license weight and actual weight matched favorably before the Lord. The DMV may have not cared, but I know God sees every dishonest tipping we do or speak.

Thinking back to the demise of Ananias and Sapphira, have you ever overstated or understated something to tip the scales in your favor? I used to tell my daughters that a half-truth is a whole lie. Ananias and Sapphira were in the congregation of those who believed. One commentary stated this husband and wife were hypocrites who faked their spirituality. Another reference stated they were believers. Christ followers sometimes tell lies. They give in to the weight of dishonest scales. What pulls scales in the wrong direction? Peter nailed the problem in Acts 5:3. Satan had filled Ananias' heart to lie to the Holy Spirit. Satan, the father of lies, wants us to lie to others because the real lie is before God. Whether others know if we are telling the truth or not, the One who made us knows every word we ever speak before it ever rolls off our tongue. He knows if our speech passes the truth test or not.

How sad that Ananias, as the head of his household, allowed his wife to be a co-conspirator in his withholding scheme. For Ananias, prophecy of Proverbs 11:19 (ESV) became a stark reality. "Whoever is steadfast in righteousness will live, but he who pursues evil will die." Sapphira followed her husband's lead, and it led her to the grave.

There was only one good repercussion of this event: The judgment from the Lord upon this husband and wife produced a great fear within the church. Imagine the impact carrying two dead bodies had on the young men who carried out the task. I bet they thought twice about the consequences of lying before they told any stories.

John Bradford, an English Reformer and martyr, coined the well-known phrase "There, but for the grace of God, goes John Bradford." Today, we substitute the personal pronoun "I." Lying is personal — and deadly. The young men who had to carry the dead bodies of Ananias and Sapphira to the graveyard had firsthand knowledge of this truth. King Solomon, one of the wisest men who ever lived, obviously knew the deadly power of lies; he specifically asked to be delivered from them. King David also asked for the way of lying to be removed from him. He knew their dire consequences. He had to bury his infant son because of lies.

Psalm 31:18 makes it clear that lying lips will be put to silence. Ananias and Sapphira never told another lie. Their lips were shut up along with their grave.

The story of Ananias and Sapphira evoked a great fear within the church of their day — and should continue to evoke fear in your heart, mine, and that of any believer who feels the need to falsely tip the scale. Here's a good verse to memorize and live by: "Lying lips are an abomination to the Lord, but those who deal truthfully are His delight" Proverbs 12:22 (NKJV).

FALSE TEACHINGS

Chapter 13 of the book of Ezekiel deals with the issue of lying. False motives produced false prophets in the days of Ezekiel. Men and women were leading the nation astray. They were producing false hope. Ezekiel challenged the source of their proclamations, knowing God was not their megaphone. In a crumbling society, people will listen to anyone who offers hope, even if it is a false one. While these men and women claimed to be God's representatives, He never endorsed them. Their false words and visions caused the Lord to be against them, not for them. They may have enjoyed the flattery of Israel's leaders for a season. However, when their prophecies proved to be false, they lost favor with everyone.

Today false motives continue to produce false prophets. When a person of authority wants to sway the thinking and the behavior of others, he or she will begin by wooing with words. Those words may appeal to what seems easy, nice, pretty, or luxurious. Let's face the truth. We all want the easiest, quickest solution to any dilemma. No one wants to face hardship to achieve a goal.

Sacrificial living isn't being taught much anymore. Smooth-talking preachers who teach only of a God who wants us to be healthy, wealthy, and wise are raking in millions. They fail to mention that a Christ follower must accept that the cross isn't just a piece of jewelry or an ornament to hang on a tree. Jesus Christ hung on the cross to set us free from sin and bondage, not to make us healthy, wealthy, and wise. Christ followers will have to suffer in this present world. The suffering should cause us to depend on Christ — not to get angry and throw Him away. Note how Kyle Idleman describes this contrast in his book *Not a Fan*.

"Contrast the symbol of the cross with our love for comfort. Most of us commit our time and resources to make our lives as comfortable as possible. We are by nature comfort seekers, not cross bearers. We are the people of the Lazyboy, the country club, the day spa, and the Snuggie… Contrast the image of the Snuggie with the image of the cross. One represents ease and comfort; the other represents pain and sacrifice. It's no surprise that more than 20 million Snuggies have been sold. Unfortunately, many churches have developed the Snuggie Theology, where they try and make sure everyone is as comfortable as possible. The Snuggie Theology promises health and wealth to all who follow Jesus. Instead of promising you a cross to carry, they promise you a luxury car and a beautiful home. The message may still be preached from the Bible in a church, but certain parts are left out, and if you look around my guess is that you won't see any crosses in the building. You start to see the consequences of the Snuggie Theology when someone's health takes a turn for the worse or their finances begin to fall apart. They start to question God because according to the gospel that was presented to them, God isn't holding up His end of the deal. One of the elders at our church described in a sentence how this happens. He said, 'What you win them with is what you win them to.' When we win them with Snuggie Theology, they are not going to be happy when they are told to take up a cross."[viii]

When preachers and teachers of the Word of God make promises that God never made, they present a false gospel. They follow their own spirits rather than the Holy Spirit. By doing so, they lead others astray with lies.

As a child I was taught to light candles for loved ones who had died without absolution from sins. By doing so, I was shortening their punishment time in the places I had learned of, and which frightened me to pieces. I wanted all my deceased aunts and uncles to be in heaven. I remember staring at the flickering candles in tears, begging God to release everyone, and allow them into heaven. Boy was I stunned to find out how false that teaching was. We are saved by grace through faith. No amount of candle burning changes our afterlife.

The prophet Jeremiah warned that trusting in lies is not profitable. Believing in a lie may bring temporary comfort, but the revealing of a lie brings extreme discomfort. How many are led astray by false words? Sadly, too many to count. Proverbs 14:12 (NKJV) makes it clear, "There is a way that seems right to a man, but its end is the way to death."

We must not listen to false doctrine. And we certainly must not teach false doctrine. There is life only in the truth found in God's Holy Word, nothing more, nothing less.

MOMENTS IN THE MIRROR

CHAPTER 5

1. As you read the story of Ananias and Sapphira, what were your thoughts?

2. Have you ever had a problem with lying? If so, what was the root cause of it?

3. What consequences have you reaped from telling lies?

4. In what areas of life are you prone to tip the scales in your favor?

5. What verse in Proverbs 11 stood out to you?

6. Have you ever twisted God's Word to make another person feel comfortable or miserable?

7. Are you familiar enough with biblical truth to distinguish when it's being misrepresented?

FIRE POKER FEAR

Sometimes, God whispers, "I've got this. Sit back and watch.

I will fight this battle for you."

I once was part of a small group nicknamed "High Counsel." We gathered every Tuesday to seek the high counsel of God for all of life's issues – marriage, children, family, church, and so forth. We offered input on issues shared by group members and prayed for one another.

At the first meeting of "High Counsel," we came up with the "Fire Poker" rule. The leader of our little tribe was sitting by her fireplace. She picked up a fire poker and stuck it in the fire. Using a stern voice, she mandated a rule: What was spoken in our small group, stayed in our small group. Anyone caught sharing "High Counsel" privacies outside the group would get the hot fire poker. She then proceeded to pull the hot poker out of the fire and thrust its red tip high for us to see. Everyone erupted in laughter, but we knew she meant business. She was a tough warrior with a strong admonition — accountability to God and one another were paramount.

To be branded by the hot poker invoked a fear in me to never break the rule. So many times I wanted to share with my husband or another person something that had been discussed in "High Counsel." However, when the memory of our leader holding up the hot poker flashed before me, I zipped my quivering lips.

THE FEAR FACTOR

Words spoken by others can instill fear in us. When spoken words create a healthy fear in us, we can be kept from wrong doing and a careless lifestyle. When toxic words spoken by others paralyze us, unhealthiness can settle into our hearts, leaving us quivering in fear. Let's take a look at some verbal warriors and the quivering they produced.

Even if you've never read the Bible, you've likely heard of a man named Goliath. Just the mention of his name conjures up an image of a burly giant with huge hands that could squeeze the life out of someone in an instant – a big guy with a well-known bad reputation. A description of Goliath is found in 1 Samuel 17 (ESV):

> " ¹Now the Philistines gathered their armies for battle. And they were gathered at Socoh, which belongs to Judah, and encamped between Socoh and Azekah, in Ephes-dammim. ² And Saul and the men of Israel were gathered, and encamped in the Valley of Elah, and drew up in line of battle against the Philistines. ³ And the Philistines stood on the mountain on the one side, and Israel stood on the mountain on the other side, with a valley between them. ⁴ And there came out from the camp of the Philistines a champion named Goliath of Gath, whose height was six cubits and a span. ⁵ He had a helmet of bronze on his head, and he was armed with a coat of mail, and the weight of the coat was five thousand shekels of bronze. ⁶ And he had bronze armor on his legs, and a javelin of bronze slung between his shoulders. ⁷ The shaft of his spear was like a weaver's beam, and his spear's head weighed six hundred shekels of iron. And his shield-bearer went before him. ⁸ He stood and shouted to the ranks of Israel, 'Why have you come out to draw up for battle? Am I not a Philistine, and are you not servants of Saul? Choose a man for yourselves, and let him come down to me. ⁹ If he is able to fight with me and kill me, then we will be your servants. But if I prevail against him and kill him, then you shall be our servants and serve us.' ¹⁰ And the Philistine said, 'I defy the ranks of Israel this day. Give me a man, that we may fight together.' ¹¹ When Saul and all Israel heard these words of the Philistine, they were dismayed and greatly afraid."

Here's the big picture: For starters, Goliath was almost ten feet tall! His head would almost touch the rim of a basketball goal. His armor weighed about 125 pounds. He carried a spear with a 15-pound iron tip. One whack on the head with that weapon would send someone into a lifelong coma. Goliath was a monster of a man, physically intimidating to say the least. His intimidation was escalated by his thunderous verbal threats. He flung them with cannonball heat. He mocked anyone who even dared to come against him. A person with good sense knew better than to belly up to Goliath.

Let's pause for a moment. In 2 Timothy 1:7 (NKJV) we're told, "For

God has not given us the spirit of fear, but of power and of love and of a sound mind." A *sound mind* can be translated *sober* or *thinking sensibly*. When we're paralyzed by fear, we often don't think soberly. We can become incapacitated by the images of intimidating people or the cannonball words they fling at us. We cower, we cave, we crumble.

I had a Goliath. Funny thing, I towered over her physically. My voice was boisterous, hers was soft. I was more of a take charge personality. She worked behind the scenes. From said description, I sound like the Goliath. However, while small in stature, and reserved in conversation, this miniature lady loomed over me like a giant. In her secret corners, she plotted my demise. One brave soul pulled me aside and issued a "beware of the bitsy giant" warning. I operated out of fear if I noticed her in a room. I avoided anywhere she may be present. Then God grabbed my attention. Through His Word I realized I was operating out of a spirit of fear, not a sound mind. I invited her to coffee. My desire – put to rest the impending doom I carried both in and out of her presence. I assured her my desire to meet was to be God honoring, yet, let her know I'd been informed of what she was saying behind my back. There were no denials or apologies, only the look of a deer in headlights. I inquired about my standing with her and what was at the root of the issue. I received no answers. But in her eyes I saw the green-eyed monster of jealousy. I chose to let her slay that Goliath. Clearly, it wasn't my assignment. I just needed to put my Goliath in her proper place – no longer looming over me. I remember the day I stood on a stage and saw her in the audience. My first inclination was to tremble. Then I remembered she was no longer a giant in my life. The Lord was protecting me. Psalm 23 flooded my mind, His rod and staff comforted me.

FISTS UP/CHESTS OUT

Now let's return to the battlefield. King Saul, the top authority, and his army, a highly trained regiment of men, were actually quivering with fear as they stared at the massive Goliath and heard his menacing threats.

Then, a young shepherd boy named David arrived on the scene. Under the direction of his father, Jesse, David had been running back and forth to bring food to his brothers, who served in Saul's army. David had to feed his brothers and protect his sheep, and he did both well. In fact, he had killed lions and bears to keep his sheep safe.

Through daily life in the fields, David had learned His God was able to deliver him from the paws of the fiercest animals. When he heard Goliath's cannonball threats, David was not intimidated; he was deeply offended. In his sober estimation, David believed God could deliver him from anything that stood in the way of God's plans for Israel's victory. So he stood before the raging Goliath armed only with confidence in God, a slingshot, and five smooth stones.

As Goliath stood there, likely laughing, he mocked his wee opponent. " 'Am I a dog, that you come to me with sticks?' And the Philistine cursed David by his gods" (1 Samuel 17:43ESV).

Undaunted by Goliath's sarcasm and curses, David uttered a huge and powerful statement:

> "You come to me with a sword and with a spear and with a javelin, but I come to you in the name of the Lord of hosts, the God of the armies of Israel, whom you have defied. **46** This day the Lord will deliver you into my hand, and I will strike you down and cut off your head. And I will give the dead bodies of the host of the Philistines this day to the birds of the air and to the wild beasts of the earth, that all the earth may know that there is a God in Israel, **47** and that all this assembly may know that the Lord saves not with sword and spear. For the battle is the Lord's, and he will give you into our hand" (1 Samuel 17:45-47).

For a moment, Goliath surely was rendered absolutely speechless by the audacity of David's words. But only for a moment. Then he charged toward David, intent on teaching the small man a brutal and life-ending lesson.

David, grounded in courage borne from his faith in God, ran toward the giant, pausing just long enough to place a small stone in his sling and whip it into the air.

The stone struck Goliath on the forehead — and the big man with the loud voice fell flat on his face, forever silenced even as his 125 pounds of armor clanged around him and the 15-pound tip of his spear dug a trench in the dirt. David then used Goliath's own sword to cut off the head of the barking giant. A small man with a big heart for God wasn't fazed by the bark of a roaring giant.

What does the story of David and Goliath teach us? A sound and sober mind sifts the words of the loud and the proud. A sound and sober mind silences intimidators. God's Word serves as a level to show what is balanced and true. The barks of a giant are rarely balanced or worth quivering over.

In times past, hospitals issued a complimentary baby photograph for the doting parents to cherish forever. I'd love to show you both of mine. Note I stated *both* of mine. The first photo depicted such a devastating terror. The camera lights must've frightened me and my face is pitiful. In the next pic, I had my fists tight and looked ready to throw a knockout punch to anyone brave enough to get near me. I've approached the giants in my life much the same way – fear or fight. Believing my anger was fierce enough to take down the brute in the opposing corner, I charged ahead. With fists up and chest out, I slung words with those knockout punches. My first Goliath just smirked and then beat me to a pulp verbally. I thought I'd never recover, but I did. I guess I'm a slow learner because I tried this tactic on another giant. Once again I crawled home with bruised emotions and decided I'd to get professional counseling. I needed to learn how to slay the giants in my life in a way which be God honoring. I want to be clear about using the word "slay". The goal is never to kill or destroy another person. The goal is to confront in the same manner David did. Go in the name of the Lord, and after much prayer. Put on your spiritual armor. Ephesians 6:13-18(The Message) describes this best. "Be prepared. You're up against far more than you can handle on your own. Take all the help you can get, every weapon God has issued, so that when it's all over but the shouting you'll still be on your feet. Truth, righteousness, peace, faith, and salvation are more than words. Learn how to apply them. You'll need them throughout your life. God's Word is an *indispensable* weapon. In the same way, prayer is essential in this ongoing warfare. Pray hard and long. Pray for your brothers and sisters. Keep your eyes open. Keep each other's spirits up so that no one falls behind or drops out."

NEGATIVE REPLAY

The day David killed loudmouthed Goliath was a turning point in history. An unknown shepherd boy became the star of the show in Israel. King Saul, who had been the tall, dark, and handsome king of Israel, was taken out of the spotlight, and David took the stage. Women danced and sang to one another as they celebrated, "Saul has slain his thousands, and David his ten thousands" 1Samuel 18:7 (NKJV).

Words replayed over and over in our minds can create a negative or positive influence. Unfortunately for Saul, the song the women sang in the streets made him second best to David and sent the king into a jealous rage. The repetitive words of comparison literally drove Saul insane because he wanted to be the center of attention. He wanted to be the hero. His big ego could not take the hit of a small man named David whose love for God and reputation for bravery were huge.

Saul didn't want women to sing about David. He wanted them to sing about him or shut up. But they kept on singing about David — and the words of the women, though truthful, festered in the heart and mind of a jealous, mentally unstable king.

James 1:8 warns that a double-minded man is unstable in all his ways. And Saul was definitely unstable. As the lyrics from the street song replayed over and over in Saul's fractured mind, he began to bark cannonball words. He ordered David to be killed — and he chased David all over the country to carry out that death sentence.

King Saul, who wore shining armor on the outside, had a dark heart churning with the poison of ego, rage, and envy. That toxic combination led to his great fall. Every time Saul hit the repeat button on the words to the street song, he hit rock bottom. The end of his life was met with tragedy. In 1 Samuel 31, Saul is up against the Philistines in battle. Three of his sons are killed, and he is severely wounded by archers. Rather than lay on the ground unprotected against the enemy, he asks his armor bearer to thrust his sword and kill him. The man refused and Saul took his own life. When the Philistines found Saul's dead body, they cut off his head (v.9). How ironic that both Saul and Goliath — who used their lofty positions, their minds, and their mouths to invoke fear — were both beheaded.

Perhaps you've encountered a Saul or Goliath before. Pray before you try to reason with, or confront them. Enlist prayer warriors to stay behind you to plead your cause before the throne of grace. If God paves the way, and your spiritual armor is secure, then go in God's strength. Sometimes, God whispers, "I've got this. Sit back and watch. I will fight this battle for you."

MAJORITY RULES

Saul was an emotionally frail man. His own insecurities, coupled with the words sung by the multitude on the street, unraveled the official ruler of

and we were like grasshoppers in our own sight, and
so we were in their sight."

Only Joshua and Caleb stated without fear that the Israelites could
overtake Canaan and the giants. The two men saw the battle as belonging to
God. (This was the same power David had proclaimed when he went up
against Goliath). Here are their words:

"The land, which we passed through to spy it out, is an exceedingly
good land. 8 If the LORD delights in us, he will bring us into this land and
give it to us, a land that flows with milk and honey. 9 Only do not rebel
against the LORD. And do not fear the people of the land, for they are
bread for us. Their protection is removed from them, and the LORD is with
us; do not fear them." Numbers 14:7-9 (ESV)

Joshua and Caleb begged the people to listen to their words, not the
fear-based words of the other spies. Joshua and Caleb were not afraid of
giants. Their confidence was based on God's power. They believed the God
who told them to go into the land would protect them and defeat the giants
that lived there.

But the majority of spies, who had little faith and lots of fear, swayed
the Israelite people, whose blood circulated with the fear of men, not the
fear of their almighty God. The backbiting and complaining reached fever
pitch. They wanted to stone Caleb and Joshua for disagreeing with the
other spies, but God protected the two brave men (Numbers 14:10).

Although Caleb and Joshua stood their ground based on faith, the ten
other spies swayed the weight of opinion through fear mongering. The
terrorizing words of the fearful majority won over the challenging words of
the faithful few. Unhealthy words spoken by unhealthy people were readily
believed by unhealthy followers.

Proverbs 14:15(NKJV) tells us, "The simple believes every word, but
the prudent considers well his steps." The Israelites had become simpletons
harnessed by fear. They believed the words of the majority even when the
majority was in error.

Some things never change. This same scenario has been repeated time
after time throughout history. Today the loud, the proud, the rich, the
famous, and those who hold the highest office get the microphone, the
spotlight, and the votes of the simpletons. Truth gets buried and lies make
headlines. Votes are cast and the minority is silenced.

After dinner, I stay glued to the nightly news, local and national. I shake my head as I observe laws which are passed daily that defy the Word of God. CEO's are ridiculed or pushed out if they voice a conservative opinion. The flamboyant lifestyles of Hollywood set the stage for what is considered culturally correct. My grandparents would turn over in their graves if they viewed half of what is permitted to air on television. Many a program has been turned off in our home for the obscenity and crude behavior which is acceptable to most families. The ratings prove the majority votes for trash. The minority has an opinion, but often gives up in defeat and silence.

SPEAK UP

We have opinions, votes, and voices. Joshua and Caleb proved opinions matter and they spoke up. Occasionally I write my congressman or senators about certain bills that are up for vote. I contact sponsors of television shows which display inappropriate content. How thrilling to see smut cancelled all because the minority wouldn't be quiet. I informed the head of a large department store selling pornographic posters on their .com site that I'd no longer be a customer. Due to the outcry of others likeminded customers, they removed the products.

Whether we are silenced or listened to, we need to speak up. We need to be wise with our words and balanced in our approach. Feet fitted with shoes of peace make a better impression than hands lifted with boxing gloves on.

MOMENTS IN THE MIRROR

CHAPTER 6

1.   In what ways do powerful people intimidate you?

2.   What kinds of words send you into a panic?

3.   Do you check out a story before you believe every word as fact?

4.   Do you go along with the crowd when casting a vote?

5.   What tactics sway your opinion?

6.   Name a time when the words of someone reverberated in your ears?

7.   Did the repetition of another's word send you into fight or flight?

PARALLEL PARKING

In the multitude of words, we can quickly wind up deficient

in character, family, and friends.

I flunked my first driver's license exam. I was a 16 at the time—and scared half out of my mind. Oh, I passed the written part just fine, but on the street, I didn't make the cut. I was driving my dad's mile-long Cadillac. I'm talking so long you could park the hood in one state and the bumper would be dragging in another. That Cadillac was a faded-gold tank that could've been used in military operations to withstand artillery. Part of the driving test required that I parallel park that thing between two other vehicles. As hard as I tried, I couldn't squeeze Ol' Bertha into that spot. I went home embarrassed but determined to learn how to park a car in the correct position.

To this day, I will park a mile away rather than parallel park. Lining up a vehicle isn't my strong, suit, so I avoid it. Lining up truth, however, is a skill I must master.

Truth and error run along parallel streets. Daily we choose which street to travel. With our mouths we speak truth or error, wisdom or foolishness. The book of Proverbs shines high-beam headlights on the differences between the wise man and the foolish man, the mouth of the wise and the mouth of the foolish. Proverbs 10 is a traveler's guide of sorts. It shows us the path of truth and the dead-end trail of lies. The parallelism between the wise man and the foolish sets the course straight for all who are willing to read, listen, and apply.

PROVERBS 10 (ESV)

"1 A wise son makes a glad father,
  but a foolish son is a sorrow to his mother.
2 Treasures gained by wickedness do not profit,
  but righteousness delivers from death.
3 The LORD does not let the righteous go hungry,
  but he thwarts the craving of the wicked.
4 A slack hand causes poverty,

but the hand of the diligent makes rich.
⁵ He who gathers in summer is a prudent son,
　but he who sleeps in harvest is a son who brings shame.
⁶ Blessings are on the head of the righteous,
　but the mouth of the wicked conceals violence.
⁷ The memory of the righteous is a blessing,
　but the name of the wicked will rot.
⁸ The wise of heart will receive commandments,
　but a babbling fool will come to ruin.
⁹ Whoever walks in integrity walks securely,
　but he who makes his ways crooked will be found out.
¹⁰ Whoever winks the eye causes trouble,
　and a babbling fool will come to ruin.
¹¹ The mouth of the righteous is a fountain of life,
　but the mouth of the wicked conceals violence.
¹² Hatred stirs up strife,
　but love covers all offenses.
¹³ On the lips of him who has understanding, wisdom is found,
　but a rod is for the back of him who lacks sense.
¹⁴ The wise lay up knowledge,
　but the mouth of a fool brings ruin near.
¹⁵ A rich man's wealth is his strong city;
　the poverty of the poor is their ruin.
¹⁶ The wage of the righteous leads to life,
　the gain of the wicked to sin.
¹⁷ Whoever heeds instruction is on the path to life,
　but he who rejects reproof leads others astray.
¹⁸ The one who conceals hatred has lying lips,
　and whoever utters slander is a fool.
¹⁹ When words are many, transgression is not lacking,
　but whoever restrains his lips is prudent.
²⁰ The tongue of the righteous is choice silver;
　the heart of the wicked is of little worth.
²¹ The lips of the righteous feed many,
　but fools die for lack of sense.
²² The blessing of the LORD makes rich,
　and he adds no sorrow with it.
²³ Doing wrong is like a joke to a fool,
　but wisdom is pleasure to a man of understanding.
²⁴ What the wicked dreads will come upon him,
　but the desire of the righteous will be granted.
²⁵ When the tempest passes, the wicked is no more,
　but the righteous is established forever.

26 Like vinegar to the teeth and smoke to the eyes,
   so is the sluggard to those who send him.
27 The fear of the LORD prolongs life,
   but the years of the wicked will be short.
28 The hope of the righteous brings joy,
   but the expectation of the wicked will perish.
29 The way of the LORD is a stronghold to the blameless,
   but destruction to evildoers.
30 The righteous will never be removed,
   but the wicked will not dwell in the land.
31 The mouth of the righteous brings forth wisdom,
   but the perverse tongue will be cut off.
32 The lips of the righteous know what is acceptable,
   but the mouth of the wicked, what is perverse."

Solomon, the son of King David, is the author of Proverbs 10. He saw and experienced the impact of both foolish and wise living. Solomon's insights instruct and exhort those who desire to live in a manner pleasing to God. The topic of the mouth weaves a common thread throughout this crash course on when to speak and what to speak.

Proverbs 10:6-7 contrasts the verbal blessings of the righteous with the verbal violence of the wicked. Note that the righteous man has blessings on his head. The literal translation has a two-fold meaning. The words the righteous man speaks, bless others. His life blesses both man and God. His words are gifts to those who hear them.

In ancient Greece, Olympic victors were crowned with laurel wreaths. Likewise, a man who uses his words to bless others will be crowned with their praises and blessings. The legacy of such a man is one of honor.

The wicked man, however, speaks violence. Luke 6:45 (NIV) warns, "… an evil man brings evil things out of the evil stored up in his heart. For the mouth speaks what the heart is full of." Imagine a toxic volcano of evil bubbling up and spewing out of an evil man! Not a pretty site. Sure, an evil person can temporarily hide and disguise evil, but eventually a jolt will spew the toxic crud smoldering beneath the surface. The mouth will display the foulness festering in a wicked man's heart, and his name will be crud. Forever.

The Greek word for eulogy is *eulogia*, which means highest praises or blessings. A blessed man is blessed in life, death, and in memories. This isn't true for the wicked. Scripture conveys that a wicked man's name will rot. Like rancid meat, his name will evoke nausea by all who remember him or even hear about him.

Proverbs 10:8 tells us the wise person has a teachable heart and listens to the words and commands of God, which lead to victory. He soaks up wise counsel and instruction given him and grows through them.

The babbling fool, on the other hand, will not listen. He is so full of idle chatter and non-stop talking that he doesn't listen or take heed to instruction. The commands of God are foolish to him and this mindset leads to ruin. His perversity is made public. Integrity is said to be what a man does in private when no one is watching. The foolish man's ways are perverse whether anyone is watching or not.

HIDDEN CAMERAS

I once had a job where cameras were installed in all rooms. Every move was on display. I was a bit "creeped out" by the roving eye that followed me. One day, I stopped and stared at the camera and its roving eye, and it dawned on me that no matter where I am, people are watching. My grown children, grandchildren, peers, and mentees are watching. Camera or no camera, our lives are on display for all to see. We are known—and will be known in the years after we are long gone—by the legacy we leave with our lives and our mouths!

In Proverbs 10:10, we learn that a babbling fool ends up falling. If babbling dominates walking, the end result is falling. Once I was chattering away to a friend while we were walking to the restroom. We were at a large conference, and the men's and women's restrooms were side by side. Since my talking dominated at that moment, I walked right into the men's restroom. Talk about a wrong turn!

A fool's walk and talk lead to the ditches of life. Proverbs 24:16 (ESV) reminds us, "For the righteous falls seven times and rises again, but the wicked stumble in times of calamity." Even when the righteous man falls, his companions will gracefully help him up. The foolish will have a hard time finding anyone to repeatedly reach into self-dug ditches.

SOUND ADVICE

Proverbs 10:13 teaches that wisdom is found on the lips of one who has understanding. At times, we all need the counsel of a wise person, someone who will be confidential, and offer clear direction using common sense and God sense. True wisdom always has a divine source. Wisdom and understanding come from the Lord and are imparted by the Lord through wise counselors.

A foolish person is incapable of imparting wisdom. We all know people who will side with us when we're hurting, but that doesn't mean those individuals are wise and qualified to communicate wisdom. Wisdom and sympathy are different things. If the heart of a sympathetic listener is not keenly tuned to the heart of God, that person's heightened emotions regarding our dilemmas can steer us in the wrong direction. And that wrong direction may be even more painful than the original dilemma. The second part of Proverbs 10:13 teaches that the foolish man's back receives the rod. Taking bad advice may lead to getting whacked in the end!

In Proverbs 10:14, we learn that the wise man stores up knowledge. What does the foolish man do? He blurts out everything he thinks. His loose lips lead to his ruination. He doesn't exercise restraint. Whatever he thinks, he assures himself is worthy of repeating.

I am so thankful that my thoughts aren't displayed over my head in a cartoon dialogue box! If others could read all my thoughts, I'd be deleted as a friend from more than just Facebook! Maturity in life, and in the Lord, has taught me verbal restraint.

Proverbs 10:19 really gets down to the business of tongue control. "When words are many, transgression is not lacking, but whoever restraints his lips is prudent." In my own life, I've learned if I keep talking and talking, I'm going to eventually damage myself or someone else. I'll end up sinning or my words may cause another to sin.

Proverbs 17:28 (ESV) makes it clear, "Even a fool who keeps silent is considered wise; when he closes his lips, he is deemed intelligent." I constantly remind myself to pause, close my mouth, take a breath, evaluate, think through, and pause again. This exercise has kept me from uttering many foolish words.

It's interesting to note that the word *selah* appears often in the Old Testament. One definition of this word is "to pause and think." If more of us took *selah* breaks, we'd avoid a lot of sinful babbling. One of my friends has coined Proverbs 10:19 as the "less is more" principle. Fewer words are more efficient. In the multitude of words, we can quickly wind up deficient in character, family, and friends.

I take a "body pump" class at a local gym. We do weights and squats and all kinds of strenuous exercises. Why? We want to be stronger and look leaner. Sometimes the strongest exercise for the mouth is to shut the muscles tight. We must not move our lips just because thoughts move through our brains. The second half of Proverbs 10:19 is powerful: "...but whoever restrains his lips is prudent." Exercising verbal restraint is a wise move.

FILTERS

Oh, to have a tongue as lovely as choice silver! That's the description of the tongue of the wise in Proverbs 10:20. Choice silver is refined through intense heat. When the refiner can see his reflection in the pure silver, then it's refined.

Words filtered through a refining process in our hearts and minds are most useful. They are even considered beautiful if they have been weighed and proven right by God. Years ago, WWJD (What Would Jesus Do?) bracelets became the rage. Today we need a WWJS (What Would Jesus Say?) version. Here's a filter I use and recommend: If Jesus wouldn't put His stamp of approval on my next verbal leakage, then I should plug it.

The wicked man doesn't filter his words. Instead, he relishes starting fires with them, and he keeps those fires kindled with more gasoline. He keeps talking. His words are cheap, but the damage they do can be costly.

Proverbs 10:21 tells us that the lips of a righteous man are like a banquet held to feed the hungry. Junk food isn't served. Only healthy and nourishing words are served.

The foolish man doesn't bother to show up for the banquet of wisdom. He stays outside and dies of malnutrition. He craves what is perverse (v. 32) and is starving outside of the hall where what is healthy is being served. Wisdom that would bring life and health is dismissed.

Here's list of additional Bible verses that contrast the ways the wise and the foolish use words.

THE WISE OR RIGHTEOUS MAN:

His words promote health. (Proverbs 12:18)

His mouth keeps his life. (Proverbs 13:3)

His words protect and preserve others. (Proverbs 14:3)

His tongue uses knowledge rightly. (Proverbs 15:2)

He studies how to answer. (Proverbs 15:28)

He teaches his mouth and adds learning to his lips. (Proverbs 16:23)

He spares his words. (Proverbs 17:27)

His words are deep waters. (Proverbs 18:4)

He has grace on his lips, the king is his friend. (Proverbs 22:11)

His words are like goads—they prod, like well driven nails. (Ecclesiastes 12:11)

THE FOOLISH OR WICKED MAN:

His mouth destroys his neighbor. (Proverbs 11:9)

His words accuse. (Proverbs 12:6)

His mouth has a rod of pride. (Proverbs 14:3)

He feeds on and pours out foolishness. (Proverbs 15:2, 14)

He digs up evil and it is on his lips like burning fire. (Proverbs 16:27)

His lips enter into contention. (Proverbs 18:6)

His mouth is his destruction and his lips the snare of his soul. (Proverbs 18:7)

He devours iniquity. (Proverbs 19:28)

He is known by his multitude of words. (Ecclesiastes 5:3)

The contrast between these two men is immeasurable. One seeks life with his words; one destroys it. The wise would cross the street to help the foolish; the foolish would refuse the help. Parallel streets do not intersect. You have to choose which street you want to travel.

MOMENTS IN THE MIRROR

CHAPTER 7

1. Would others say that your words bless them?

2. What prompts critical words in your dialogue with others?

3. What person/persons will one day speak your eulogy? What do you think they will say about you?

4. Is there anyone you wouldn't want to speak at your funeral? If so, why?

5. Would you say you have a teachable heart? Or do you tend to be stubborn when given wise advice?

6. If a hidden camera and recorder followed you for a week, would you be satisfied with your speech and conversations? Would God?

7. Do you tend to speak run-on sentences and babble? Or do you pause for others to interact?

8. Are you in the habit of reflecting on what you're saying, how it may come across, or if you need to end certain conversations?

9. Do you agree with the "less is more" principle?

NAUGHTY OR NICE

Only His power can transform a naughty mouth into a nice one.

I smile when I think of my kindergarten days. I was blessed with the sweetest teacher any five-year-old could ask for, Mrs. George. When I was growing up, kindergarten was the first exposure to breaking away from mom's immediate presence. Often on the first day of kindergarten, a child would clutch the coat of his or her mom and scream not to be left. Mrs. George would bend down and whisper a little secret in that distraught child's ear. She had a big jar of M&M's that would soothe in an instant. Soon enough, the cries would stop and all was well with the world.

Kindhearted Mrs. George was not a pushover, however. When a child acted up, our teacher would become the firm escort to the infamous territory known as the naughty corner. I was a high achiever, and to me that corner represented shame. I did my best to stay out of it. I worried about the naughty corner more than any five-year-old should have.

At times, I still worry more than I should. I have little power over many things that concern me. However, there are things I do have power over through Christ. One of those is the power to choose to speak in a naughty or nice manner.

I didn't surrender my life to Christ until I was 21, so my college days were on the wild side and included a potty mouth. I'm not proud of my behavior back then, but the greatest thing about my past is that it's in the past! God has forgiven my wild past, and He has allowed my testimony to help others struggling with bad behavior. Today, I'm a trophy of God's grace. Only He can change a life. Only His power can transform a naughty mouth into a nice one.

What constitutes a naughty mouth and does God have anything to say about foul language? Truth is, He has a lot to say about it.

"Let there be no filthiness nor foolish talk nor crude joking, which are out of place, but instead let there be thanksgiving." Eph. 5:4 (ESV)

"No foul language is to come from your mouth, but only what is good for building up someone in need, so that it gives grace to those who hear." Eph. 4:29 (HCSB)

"Like a madman...is the man who deceives his neighbor and says, 'I am only joking!' " Prov. 26:19 (ESV)

"But now you must put them all away: anger, wrath, malice, slander, and obscene talk from your mouth." Col. 3:8 (ESV)

BLUSHING

I must confess that although my potty mouth has been cleansed by the blood of Jesus, sometimes it still needs a good flushing. I've told jokes that I later apologized for. I've used words that offended others. I've emailed some stories that made me blush and then persuaded myself they weren't too bad to pass around.

If my words or stories make another person blush, then I'm reverting to my past behavior. The Bible actually addresses blushing. I guess God designed blushing as a built-in sensor to let us know when we've said, heard, or done something that's inappropriate.

In Jeremiah Chapter 8, the children of Israel were in a perpetual state of backsliding. The prophet declares God's anger against the offenses of the people. Verse 12 (KJV) gets right to the heart of the matter: "Were they ashamed when they had committed abomination? No! They were not at all ashamed, nor did they know how to blush..."

Blushing is the body's way of showing emotion. To not blush when you've heard or spoken something that's crude, demonstrates immunity to what offends God. Psalm 24:4 talks about coming to God with clean hands and a pure heart. No doubt about it, He also desires a clean mouth.

Job 6:30 (KJV) asks some thought-provoking questions: "Is there injustice on my tongue? Cannot my taste discern the unsavory?" What if every time a cuss word or other unsavory language rolled off our tongues, we tasted ten-day-old dead fish? Would we change our vocabulary or the jokes we tell? How does it sound to those around us if in one breath we praise God and in the next we spew filthy words? James 3:10-12 (KJV) makes the irony of the conflict clear: "Out of the same mouth proceed blessing and cursing. My brethren, these things ought not to be so. Does a spring send forth fresh water and bitter from the same opening? Can a fig tree, my brethren, bear olives, or a grapevine bear figs? Thus no spring yields both salt water and fresh."

A NIGHT AT THE MOVIES

When our daughters were young, we had a family rule about going to the movies. We left the theater if the language included certain words. If the Lord's name was used in a damning way, we left. We never wanted to condone filthy language. If the Lord commands us to not take His name in vain, He doesn't want us to enjoy entertainment that includes it.

Several years ago, my neighbor's son, 4-years-old at the time, used to visit me. He wasn't really coming to see me as much as to feast from the candy dish I had on my coffee table. He was the cutest red-haired boy with impish charm I couldn't resist. On one of his visits as he crunched on the candy, he blurted an expletive that stunned me. When I asked him where he learned the bad word, he told me he'd heard it in a movie he had watched.

What we hear gets stored in our memory banks. That innocent 4-year-old's memory bank withdrew a word deposited the night before and dispensed it from his lips. That particular deposit was an unhealthy one. Unfortunately, some deposits are etched with contaminated ink. The withdrawals from those deposits retain the contaminated ink, staining anyone they touch. Contaminated deposits must be permanently sealed. Psalm 141:3 (NLT) reminds us to "Take control of what I say, O LORD, and keep my lips sealed."

Ephesians 5:4 (ESV) sets the verbal standard: "Let there be no filthiness nor foolish talk nor crude joking, which are out of place..." We all love a good joke and a hearty laugh, but when does a joke become crude? I tend to believe if we blush when we tell or hear jokes, then the jokes may (notice I said *may*) fall in the coarse or crude category. A good rule of thumb is to ask, *would I tell a particular joke or story if Jesus were in the crowd? Would He laugh?*

What about those four letter words we learn are no-no's as children — the ones that connect a mouth with a bar of soap? On weekends, my husband and I like to relax with a rental movie and a bowl of buttered popcorn. The hardest part of renting a movie is finding one that sounds funny or interesting only to note the bad rating because of crude language. We often go to the rental box and leave empty handed. If movie humor isn't humorous to God, is it humorous at all? God cares about what we think is funny.

HAND PROTECTION

In Psalm 141:3, David asks God to put a guard over his mouth and to watch over the door of his lips. Job made the same request. He was tried and tested to the limits of sanity. In his powerless and pitiful state, he questioned God. He basically shook his fist at God for ever allowing him to be born. Only after God revealed His sovereignty did Job say in Chapter 40:5 (KJV), "Behold I am vile; what shall I answer you? I lay my hand over my mouth."

If laying our hands over our mouths rescues us from saying anything vile, then by all means we should do it!

James 1:26 (NKJV) tell us, "If anyone among you thinks he is religious, and does not bridle his tongue but deceives his own heart, this one's religion is useless." James makes it clear that the occasional hand over the mouth won't work for some of us. A bridle may be required for constant control. When inserted in a horse's mouth, the bridle and bit guide the horse. Sometimes I sense a heavenly tug when my mouth is about to utter something that could make a conversation go wayward. Surrendering my mouth to God for constant control is the best way to stay on the right track. If I sense the bridle steering me from naughty to nice, I yield to the one doing the yanking!

I'd like to make a confession here. I have family and friends who think certain off color topics are funny, and laughing along with them is much easier than ducking out of a conversation. What are we supposed to do when a conversation makes us feel uncomfortable? Is there a way to turn the topic around without embarrassing those "cutting up and letting loose?" In moments like this, we need to stop and ask God what is the wisest move we can make. If slipping out and heading to the restroom is all we can think of, then by all means we need to take that exit.

My husband and I have best friends, David and Bonnie. Our first outing with them as new acquaintances was to a play. I made the choice after reading reviews stating, "Side splitting laughter." The acting was great and the music – terrific! After the first scene though, the jokes were teetering on the crude side. Hoping the dialogue would get better, I kept my mouth shut. At intermission, I hoped my friends would say they were feeling a bit uncomfortable and were okay with leaving. They kept quiet. I convinced myself I was always the prude and silenced the little voice inside. By the end of the play I wanted to run out of the theater. On the way home I apologized for not bowing out earlier in the evening. Everyone had the same sentiments. They wanted to spare my feelings since I had picked the play. Each one of us, in an effort to not step on another's toes, kept quiet. We learned about each other that evening, our likes and dislikes, and the standards we wanted to maintain. We promised to speak up if we were feeling uncomfortable. Often times, sparing feelings doesn't make us better people or cause us to grow. With David and Bonnie, we have matured in friendship because of our mutual and gentle honesty. Find friends to grow up with, and old with.

MOMENTS IN THE MIRROR

CHAPTER 8

1. Have you ever indulged in risqué humor?

2. If so, was the naughty humor something you watched or verbally participated in?

3. Have you ever blushed at another person's jokes? your own jokes?

4. Do you have a filter system for what words are acceptable from your mouth?

5. What is your guideline for naughty or nice speech?

6. Would you change your speech or conversations if Jesus were present?

7. What words do you think should be eliminated from your vocabulary?

TURTLES AND RABBITS

The Bible was not written for any of us to use as a hammer.

The older I get, the more I appreciate the vast wisdom found in the simplicity of children's stories. Remember Aesop's fable *The Tortoise and the Hare?* The braggart rabbit is quick to tell the plodding turtle that speed always wins. But the rabbit snoozes and loses even though he turns on the speed at the end of the race.

I've learned the hard way there are times when being quick isn't the right move, especially when it relates to words. My quick tongue has wounded others more times than I care to admit. Several years ago I taught Sunday school for a large group of women. Too often the women would get lengthy in their prayer needs. For the sake of time, I would try to speed along their verbiage with my perfunctory solution to their dilemmas and then tack on a prayer line. I handled my need for speed in poor fashion. As a result, one woman left the class. She hadn't felt heard or cared for.

It's not only a plethora of words that can cause problems. I've often wished that I had paused and thought through the ramifications of a request before uttering the single word "Yes." And there have been times my quick and defiant "No!" has left me filled with regret.

The Tortoise and the Hare closes with these words, "Slowly does it every time!" Some versions say, "Slow and steady wins the race." Taking the time to pray and seek God's face before speaking either a single word or a diatribe may save a relationship, a job, or even choice of the right life direction.

Seven words found in James 1:19 say a lot about word restraint: "...let every man be slow to speak..." And Proverbs 29:20 (ESV) doesn't mince words when it comes to speed talking: "Do you see a man who is hasty in his words? There is more hope for a fool than for him."

Tortoise slow is the wise way to go when it comes to speaking.

THE LONG REGRET OF HASTY WORDS

When I was a young bride, I learned through a tragic incident how devastating hasty words can be. My husband and I returned home one night to find two police cars in our driveway. An officer immediately began asking us how well we knew our neighbors, who had a heated argument earlier that evening. The wife discovered her husband had taken her paycheck and bought drugs and alcohol, leaving no money to pay bills or buy food. Apparently this had become a habit for him. She kicked him out of the house and told him she wished he were dead.

Sadly, her words were prophetic. The man fled the house, tried to cross the highway in his drunken stupor, and was hit by a semi-truck. He died at the scene.

The police officers asked us to help them tell our neighbor about her husband's death. Then we took her to the hospital to identify his body. The poor woman sobbed in anguish during the entire drive to the hospital. Her last words to her husband were hasty, horrible words spoken in anger. She would regret uttering them for the rest of her life.

Job was a man closely acquainted with the pain of anguish. And he was a man who knew the bitter taste of regretted words. When we read the early chapters of the Book of Job, we quickly realize that this godly man had lost just about everything: his wealth, his children, and his health. Things got so bad Job's wife actually told him to "Curse God and die!" (Job 2:9).

Though he was racked by grief and confusion and in terrible physical pain, Job still chose his words wisely. Even when his wife gave him horrible advice, he replied with calm and wisdom, "You are talking like a foolish woman. Shall we accept good from God, and not trouble?" (Job 2:10 NIV).

Word obviously spread that Job had hit hard times. When the going gets tough, we all like to think we can lean on our friends for support. Job had three friends who traveled from their homes to sympathize with him and comfort him: Eliphaz, Bildad, and Zophar. They sat in ashes with him for seven days and didn't utter a word because they grasped the depth of his suffering. For a while, their silent presence spoke far more to Job than any words they could speak. They were simply there for their friend. (Job 2:11-13)

We are not told what eventually caused Job to lose hope, but in Job 3 he does lose it. His pain directs his thoughts and words. He questions why God ever allowed him to be born (Job 3:11). The silence that had settled over the room was broken. Eventually, his friends started questioning, accusing, and chastising Job for his "unknown" sin. Their slant? Job must have done something to bring on that much suffering.

Job's friend's accusations accelerated his downward spiral. He begins to question the mercy of God, proving that pain-directed speech like that of his friends causes more pain.

In Chapter 20(NKJV), Job's friend Zophar argued with Job and proclaimed, "My anxious thoughts make me answer, because of the turmoil within me." Zophar was going to bust a gut until he spoke his mind about Job's dilemma. Zophar wanted to beat Job to the finish line with accusations. Later in Chapter 32, a man named Elihu enters the scene to confront the suffering servant. He declares he is full of words like wine ready to burst from new wineskins. As new wine ferments it has to have a vent. Elihu believed his wisdom was so grand that he just had to vent it. Unfortunately, his arrogance far exceeded his wisdom.

Proverbs 12:18 (NKJV) tell us that the tongue of the wise promotes health. Verse 20 reveals "counselors of peace have joy." Proverbs 12:25 (NKJV) makes it clear, "Anxiety in the heart of a man causes depression, but a good word makes it glad." Job wasn't healthier or happier after his so-called friends summed up their accusatory speeches. Good words were not spoken in a peaceful manner.

I, too, have spoken words of folly, spouting off Bible verses to show someone the error of their ways. Later, the Lord showed me the way I handled the situation put another person down. The Bible was not written for any of us to use as a hammer.

THE LAST WORD

The tirades of Job's friends lasted a lot longer than his verbal outburst about wishing he had never been born. In Chapter 6:3, Job confesses he has been rash with his mouth.

Isn't this the same thing that happens to us? We speak first and realize the frivolity of our words second. Several verses later Job asks for help to hold his tongue. We all should pray this prayer daily!

In Job 40, the Almighty speaks up. God basically asks Job if he has the right or authority to "correct the Almighty."

Job's response? Shame. His first desire was to put his hand over his mouth for speaking in haste. Smart move.

Hasty accusations usually aren't tasty ones. We don't want to regurgitate them. As God spews questions at Job like water from a fire hydrant, Job is silenced. He is slow of speech — and for good reason. In Chapter 42(ESV), Job is humbled by the greatness of his God. He repents of his verbal insolence. He confesses that he "uttered what he did not understand" (verse 3).

In verse 5, with a broken and contrite heart, Job asks God to listen to his humble confession: "I had heard of you by the hearing of the ear, but now my eyes see You." Job had believed in God, yet wavered at the Almighty's sovereignty during affliction. When Job came to his senses, he finally knew God as the Most High God. Majestic. Sovereign. Omniscient.

John MacArthur notes, "All that was left for Job to do was repent! The ashes upon which the broken man sat had not changed, but the heart of God's suffering servant had. Job did not need to repent of some sin which Satan or his accusers had raised. But Job had exercised presumption and allegations of unfairness against his Lord and hated himself in a way that called for brokenness and contrition."[ix]

As for all the questions God posed, Job had no response. Those profound questions put Job in his place. They allowed him to catch a vision of God's glory, which is unquestionable and answerable!

Frederick M. Lehman wrote a song entitled "The Love of God." In trying to describe the Almighty's love, Lehman's lyrics spoke of oceans filled with ink, quills soaking the ink and writing across the sky. His conclusion – there'd not be enough ink or sky to illustrate the love of God. There aren't enough words in any language to express the love of God, the majesty of God, or the wisdom of God.

Job was silenced by the Almighty's inquiry. When he opened his mouth, Job abhorred the words he had spoken about God. Though he did not ask for a second chance, God freely gave the broken man a second half of life more abundant than the first.

As for the friends of Job, God was not pleased with their arrogance and accusations against Job. No sin had caused Job's misfortune. The suffering servant was vindicated by God. Job's friends were chastised by God for the error of their ways and their words. Chapter 42:8 continues with an admonition, "Now therefore take seven bulls and seven rams and go to my servant Job and offer up a burnt offering for yourselves. And my servant Job shall pray for you, for I will accept his prayer not to deal with you according to your folly. For you have not spoken of me what is right, as my servant Job has."

Our Creator is concerned about our thoughts and words portraying who He is. If we speak about Him with an arrogant spirit to put down or shut up another person, God is not pleased. He is listening to our words and watching the attitudes of our hearts.

BEHIND THE SCENES

In Acts 18, a man named Apollos was preaching about the Lord in the synagogue. His limited knowledge stopped at the point of the baptism of John. Apollos didn't understand that Jesus was the Messiah who fulfilled all that was prophesied. God didn't chastise Apollos because the eager evangelist's only desire was to make God known. Instead, God allowed two believers, Aquilla and Priscilla, to come along side Apollos and teach him the rest of the story. He went on to proclaim all of the truth boldly.

Serving as godly counselors, Aquilla and Priscilla spoke wise words and equipped a man to be a kingdom builder. Had they chastised Apollos for not teaching all of the truth or belittled him for not knowing the rest of the story, Apollos may have become as discouraged as Job.

Words build up and words tear down. Job's friends sinned because they presumed to know the sum of what was going on — and voiced their opinions accordingly. Their words further wounded their suffering friend. They based their reasoning on limited earthly perspective with no clue about what was transpiring in the heavenly realm.

Far too often we do the same. We fail to slow our roll and to ask God for godly wisdom. We see circumstances through distorted lenses and frame thoughts with worldly wisdom that relies on the senses. If we open our mouths before we fall to our knees, we may sin or cause others to sin.

When God spoke to Job's friends, He called their words and actions folly. *Nĕbalah*, the Hebrew word for "folly" means "senselessness, a disgrace." These friends thought they were sensible. God thought otherwise! Senselessness leaves out the heavenly and is blind to the powers of an all-powerful God.

The beauty of Job's second half of life reads as follows:

> " Now the LORD blessed the
> latter days of Job more than his
> beginning; for he had fourteen
> thousand sheep, six thousand camels,

one thousand yoke of oxen, and one thousand female donkeys. [13] He also had seven sons and three daughters. [14] And he called the name of the first Jemimah, the name of the second Keziah, and the name of the third Keren-Happuch. [15] In all the land were found no women so beautiful as the daughters of Job; and their father gave them an inheritance among their brothers. [16] After this Job lived one hundred and forty years, and saw his children and grandchildren for four generations. [17] So Job died, old and full of days. Job 42:12-18 (NKJV)

Can you imagine the speechlessness of Job's friends when God so richly blessed him? Haven't we all dropped our jaws when God's vibrant majesty took over where our senselessness paled? Haven't we all had to repent of leaving God out of the equation? Haven't we all apologized to someone for speaking rashly without consulting the Creator?

Even when God seems to make no sense, we are foolish to assume we have the wisdom to explain anything. We have no idea what is transpiring in heaven on our behalf. Ecclesiastes 5:2 (NKJV) is a filled with powerful verbal wisdom. It is a verse we must commit to memory and apply to our tongues every day:

"Do not be rash with your mouth, And let not your heart utter anything hastily before God. For God is in heaven, and you on earth; therefore let your words be few."

MOMENTS IN THE MIRROR

CHAPTER 9

1. Recall a time in your life when you spoke quickly. Did you later regret the advice you gave or the conversation you had?

2. Who was wounded in the process and why?

3. When was the last time you left God out of the equation?

4. Have you ever made decisions based on what made sense before seeking God's face?

5. What person could you identify with most in the story of Job?

OPEN "MIC" NIGHT

There can be no healing where there is no revealing.

Monday nights are open "mic" night at a nearby coffee house. Brave souls wait their turn to sing, play an instrument, or recite some form of reading for entertainment. The house is packed on this special night. Or should I say it is filled to overflow with observers and supporters of the brave souls who dared to venture up to a microphone that is turned on? Public speaking is one of the most commonly reported social fears. I once heard a comedian say the second most dreaded fear is dying. Hence, most people would rather be in a coffin than giving their own eulogy. Speaking up or out is difficult for the shy, inhibited type. Add a microphone to the equation and you see people shrivel up or slither down to become unseen. Don't you remember those school days when a teacher would unexpectedly call on you for an answer? Your face blushed beet red, your hands went sweaty, or worse your underarms let loose and made a ring on shirt that people watched grow from across the classroom. Only the smarty-pants threw up their hands to belt out answers. Most folks just preferred to fade into the scenery hoping to not be noticed.

A famous Scottish proverb states that open confession is good for the soul. If the proverb is true, then why do most people dread opening their mouths to say or speak anything in front of even an audience of one? Anonymity breeds silence. Open confession calls attention to the person speaking and what they are speaking about. This is when most people adopt the "silence is golden" proverb instead. Is open confession really therapeutic as stated by the Scot who coined the phrase?

CONFESSION

The definition of "confess" is to tell or make known (as something wrong or damaging to oneself). The Biblical definition carries the meaning to shoot, throw, or cast down. Forgive my next analogy, but I think it is relevant to understand the meaning of confession. If you have ever eaten something that didn't settle well in your digestive track, you probably started feeling nauseous. Perhaps saliva began to rush to your mouth followed by your undigested food. While the whole scenario was unpleasant from start to finish, you later felt relieved everything had thrown up or cast out. Confession is throwing or casting out something that is wreaking havoc in your soul. Stored iniquities become infirmities which can eventually eat at our bodies, our spirits, and our souls (home of the mind, will, and emotions). Confession that owns up to truth, and is relayed with sincerity, becomes a healing agent to the inner man. To remain silent is damaging.

In Psalm 32:3, David states that his body was wracked with pain when he refused to confess his sin. In the South we would say, "It tore him plumb up!" Unconfessed sin is bottled up poison. There can be no healing where there is no revealing. When physical pain in the body is ignored, the results can be traumatic. Preventative maintenance is better than critical care hospitalization. Remember what Adam and Eve did when they sinned in the garden? They hid from God in fear and shame. At night they must've lain sleepless on the forest floor knowing that God would show up at any time. They tried to cover themselves with fig leaves (as if that would somehow cover their sin as well). Fig leaves and excuses wasn't what God was looking for. He wanted them to confess and come clean. Their disobedience was sinful. Trying to hide from God, making excuses, and telling lies were their spiral downward. I wonder what the outcome would've been if Adam and Eve had cried out to God the moment they ate the infamous "apple"?

So, when is confession good? When is confession not good? To answer that let's check out what the Creator of life has to say.

Leviticus 5:5-6 (NKJV) addresses the issue of confession, "And it shall be, when he is guilty in any of these [matters], that he shall confess that he has sinned in that [thing]; 'and he shall bring his trespass offering to the LORD for his sin which he has committed, a female from the flock, a lamb or a kid of the goats as a sin offering. So the priest shall make atonement for him concerning his sin."

The matter being addressed in Leviticus was dealing with a person who had sworn, or spoke thoughtlessly with his lips. If he had taken a vow and not kept it and suddenly realized his sin, he was to first confess and then make an offering. We need to be aware when we have sinned. Stuffing, hiding, and pretending are incubators for guilt. God is cognizant of our sin before we ever feel guilt or remorse. The Almighty has designed us with a conscience.

In the eighth chapter of John, a group of religious leaders bring a woman to Jesus. She had been caught in the act of adultery. Moses said the penalty for this sin should be stoning the person to death. The leaders asked Jesus if the woman should be stoned. Jesus replied to the men, "He who is without sin among you, let him throw a stone at her first." What was the men's response? Verse 9(NKJV) states: "Then those who heard it, being convicted by their conscience, went out one by one, beginning with the oldest, even to the last." Each man's conscience had convicted him of his individual sin. What a pity they walked away without confessing to the very One who would forgive them just for the asking. 1 John 1:9-10(ESV) "If we confess our sins, He is faithful and just to forgive us our sins and cleanse us from all unrighteousness. If we say that we have not sinned, we make Him a liar, and His word is not in us." Confession is not only good for the soul; it is cleansing and healing as well. Taking a bath or shower not only feels good, it is cleansing and healthy for the body. To not take a bath or shower is unhealthy and becomes offensive to those within close proximity. Not confessing sin has a ripple effect. Guilt eats on the unrepentant or un-disclosing soul. The wake is felt by anyone who gets too close to the water's edge of conviction.

COUPON CONVICTION

I once made a poor decision in a grocery store line. While pulling out all my coupons, I noticed the one for my ice cream had expired. At first, I was frustrated for letting it expire. Next, I justified that I had planned to shop the day before and would've used the coupon then. So why not just use it today and pretend I didn't know it expired? All of this sounded pretty harmless as I rationalized the sin in my mind. I also thought if the cashier didn't notice the expiration date it would be her fault, not mine. Sure enough, the cashier didn't notice and I got my ice cream for such a great bargain. As I was walking out to my car the Lord convicted me of dishonesty. I felt the Spirit nudging me to go back in and confess to the cashier. I tried to argue with God but we know that is pointless. So I marched back with my ice cream in hand and got behind a woman with a grocery cart piled as high as Mt. Everest (well almost). When I looked the cashier in the face and told her about the expired coupon she began to weep. In her broken Russian/English she explained how she had to pay out of her own pocket any expired coupons she had overlooked. In tears, I apologized and tried to give her the money for the coupon cost. She told me she was unable to do the transaction and that I had to take care of the matter at the customer service desk. Once again, I had to confess to another group of people. Truthfully, I wanted to lay down the money and run, but I knew God was teaching me an impacting lesson. Secret sin is not sweet. The open confession allowed a sweetness to be restored between myself and the Lord. No coupon or ice cream was worth the high cost of that confession.

LATE CONFESSIONS

Joshua was a man chosen by God to lead the Israelites to the Promised Land. God miraculously parted the Jordan River so he and the Israelites could cross over. Later, God supernaturally worked through Joshua and his army to defeat Jericho and tear down its mighty walls. The next incident that happened caught Joshua by surprise. Instead of God mightily whipping the enemies at the next place of battle for Joshua's army, God allowed them to be defeated. With a broken heart, Joshua pleads with God to find out why He has removed His hand of blessing from Israel. God answers Joshua by revealing that one of his men had sinned and brought transgression among the people. One of Joshua's men, Achan, had stolen some plunder from Jericho which had been forbidden. He had buried the treasures in the earth below his tent. Joshua had the painful duty of finding out who committed the sin. When Achan was found out Joshua's counsel was "My son, I beg you, give glory to the Lord God of Israel, and make confession to Him, and tell me now what you have done; do not hide it from me." (Joshua 7:19)

Note the order of confessing. First, Achan was to confess to God, and then to Joshua. This thief only confessed when he was forced to. He relayed what he'd done to both God and Joshua. He needed to repent before God, but because his sin affected and infected God's people, Achan also had to tell Joshua before the tribes of Israel. James 5:16 (ESV) tells us, "Therefore, confess your sins to one another and pray for one another, that you may be healed." Only when Achan's open confession was made could there be healing for the children of Israel. Joshua was next in line to hear Achan's confession since the sin affected all in Joshua's charge. We need to confess to the person we have wronged as the Lord directs us. Achan's confession was too late for his offense. His transgression carried a high price – the penalty of death. Confession may lead to forgiveness, but the weight of the sin may carry consequences you are unable to bear.

I would like to add a word of caution in referencing James 5:16 about confessing to one another. When the soul can no longer carry the weight of our sin, we need to be wise to whom we confess. We need to confess to the wronged party but at the right time. We need to find safe people to encourage and pray for us as we head into confession.

Henry Nouwen quotes, "We probably have wondered in our many lonesome moments if there is one corner in this competitive, demanding world where it is safe to be released, to expose ourselves to someone else, and to give unconditionally. It might be very small and hidden. But if this corner exists, it calls for a search through the complexities of our human relationships in order to find it."ˣ

Safe people are hard to find. They are a rare treasure not located on any map. You search souls as you journey through relationships. You test the waters to see if people are shallow or deep. Sometimes you have to take risks. In my journey through life and friendships I have risked and been burned. I've share intimacies with "friends" I thought were secret keepers and been scorched. I didn't give up though. I kept searching for the corners that Nouwen mentioned until I found safe beings. I know God brought these people to me for my growth and His glory.

Larry Crabb has great insight on this matter. "Indeed, we need spiritual friends, broken people who will provide safety for us to be broken, caring people who want us to live and believe we can live well, giving people who pour the life they have received from God into us, people of vision who see the Spirit shaping us into the image of Christ. Without them we settle for so much less."ˣⁱ

Cody Smith lists the benefits of mutual confession:

• Spoken out, our sins first become more real to us. A slight pang of guilt so easily rationalized or ignored is now named for what it really is, an affront to God.

• Hidden sin is a stronghold of Satan in our lives. He uses our failures, and especially our repeated failures to accuse us of our unworthiness as a disciple. Confession breaks this hold over us.

• Perhaps the greatest human need, one that we all share, is to be able to take off our mask, and be known and accepted by others just as we truly are. The fear of being known however, often denies us the very relationships that we long for.

• The discovery that we are not alone, our personal struggles are usually much more common than they are unique.

• The people around you already know about most of your weaknesses, imagine how their opinion of you will soften when you begin to agree with the obvious.

• The power of unified prayer can bring us the grace to

become changed.[xii]

Smith also states, "Confession shines the light of truth on our brokenness and invites others to join us in our struggle. By becoming accountable to others the crisis of change is upon me; now that I am known, I obviously can't go on forever confessing the same sins to the same people, my own pride begins to work on my behalf." [xiii]

Safe people will encourage us to journey deep inside ourselves, to find the hidden places that need exposure and confession. This process leads to healing. With the "mic" turned on, the volume set low, we can open our mouths and confess secret sins that God will begin to heal. The outcome of the confession belongs to God. The responsibility of confessing belongs to you and to me.

Let the journey begin!

MOMENTS IN THE MIRROR

CHAPTER 10

1. Name a time you refused to confess a sin.

2. Why did you keep the sin a secret?

3. Have you ever tried to justify a sin only to keep a gnawing feeling deep inside?

4. Have you ever had to confess to God AND another person?

5. Do you have a safe person to confess your sins to? If so, why did you choose that person as your safe haven?

6. What work in your life do you need to do to become a safe person?

7. Are you in the habit of daily confession before God?

A STEADFAST GUARD

The condition of our heart directly affects each and every conversation we have.

In 1995, my husband and I went on a mission trip to Russia, where we trained Russian educators to teach the Bible in public schools. For two weeks, we poured out our lives and our hearts to see the kingdom of God expanded. It was a life-changing experience.

Our return trip home included a one-day layover in London. Watching "Changing the Guard at Buckingham Palace" was at the top of our must-see list. With stoic faces and fully loaded rifles, The Queen's Guard protects The British Monarchy. Highly skilled soldiers of valor, these men are operational troops, most of whom have served in Iraq or Afghanistan. They are not simply on display for the fancy of Her Majesty Queen Elizabeth or as a tourist attraction. Their mission is to guard the lives of The Royal Family.

THE MOUTH AND HEART CONNECTION

Oh, how helpful it would be to have loyal guards protecting my mouth, saving me from dangerous words — mine and those of others! One of the Hebrew words for *guard* is *shamar, which denotes saving life.* Proverbs 21:23 (NKJV) tells us, "Whoever guards his mouth and tongue keeps his soul from troubles." And Proverbs 4:23 (NIV) tells us, "Above all else, guard your heart, for everything you do flows from it." One verse warns to guard the mouth; the other extols guarding the heart. Are the mouth and heart connected? Absolutely.

In 1 Thessalonians 5:23, Paul admonishes believers to be sanctified in body, soul, and spirit. The soul is the seat of the mind, will, and emotions. It houses thinking, feeling and doing. With our minds, we think thoughts. With our hearts, we feel emotions. And with our will, we act out what we're thinking and feeling. It's a serious connection.

As a child, I sang the song "Dem Bones." The lyrics speak of the finger bone connected to the hand bone, the hand bone connected to the arm bone, and so forth. In the spiritual realm, the mouth bone is connected to the mind and heart. When the mind volleys a thought back and forth, the emotions of the heart quickly make contact. As the emotions take up volleying, the will enters the game. And when will takes control, the mouth speaks.

Imagine you're in a group setting — workplace, Sunday school, small group — when the leader says something that sounds derogatory against you. Your mind begins to race with what was uttered. You mentally deliberate: *Am I being overly sensitive? Could I be mistaken that his words were directed to me?* Then your heart gets entangled with your thoughts. You feel hurt and angry, believing that you became a spectacle at this person's whim. At this point, your will becomes involved. You retaliate with a verbal barb. This is when your will and mouth are synchronized.

Psalm 19:14 (ESV) is a much-needed prayer to guard both the mouth and the heart: "Let the words of my mouth and the meditation of my heart be acceptable in Your sight, O LORD, my rock and my Redeemer." The wisdom of the prayer is back up by Proverbs 16:23 (KJV) "The heart of the wise teaches his mouth, and adds learning to his lips."

The Queen's Guard prevents evil doers from entering Buckingham Palace and doing The Royal Family harm. Likewise, the guards we place over our hearts will keep evil from sneaking in and doing harm. Should evil forge its way into our hearts, our mouths will also spew evil.

Luke 6:45 (NKJV) makes the heart-mouth connection explicit: "A good man out of the good treasure of his heart brings forth good; and an evil man out of the evil treasure of his heart brings forth evil. For out of the abundance of the heart his mouth speaks." James 3:6 (NKJV) back up this truth: "And the tongue is a fire, a world of iniquity. The tongue is so set among our members that it defiles the whole body, and sets on fire the course of nature; and it is set on fire by hell."

Here's the sobering, unfiltered truth that should render us speechless: The condition of our hearts directly affects each and every conversation we have.

JOB'S WIFE SPEAKS

Earlier we took a peek into the life of Job. Now, let's look at his wife. In Job 2:9, she speaks to her husband, holding nothing back: "Do you still hold fast to your integrity? Curse God and die!"

Granted, this woman was experiencing the worst days of her life. She was shocked, hurt, and angry. She was used to a life where she had it all —

a prosperous husband, a large and close- knit family, wealth, and the world at her fingertips. Then, in just a few days, there was little left of the world she had known.

I've never had days that came close to this woman's experience. My heart has never absorbed that much agony. However, I have known intense grief and anguish. I've been on the verge of collapsing under the weight of pain, and I've questioned God, just as Job did. But what I deeply grieve as I read this wife's charge to her husband are the four words "curse God and die."

There was a time in my life when I experienced abject rejection by the person I loved most in the world. Hurt and anger penetrated my heart. I asked God why He allowed painful circumstances to enter my life. In a moment of deep hurt and anxiety, I had the audacity to say to God, *"If this is how You treat me after all I have done to serve You, I'm putting You on a shelf. I'll try things on my own for a while."*

I came extremely close to cursing God as Job's wife did. Like her, I had gotten accustomed to an idealistic life. When God allowed crashing waves to level my sand castle, I was angry — and offended.

Serving God and loving God feels great when we live on easy street, but this mindset reflects shallow living and shallow thinking — and heart problems. Psalm 62:10 tells us that if our riches increase we shouldn't set our heart on them. Matthew 6:21 warns, "Where your treasure is, there your heart will be also."

Did Job's wife drift into loving her things more than her God? I won't condemn her, for I'm not sure if she spoke out of momentary grief or the actual condition of her heart. I do know this, if my mind isn't set on the truth that God is good in spite of my circumstances, I can fall into Mrs. Job's trap. This is why Colossians 3:2 tells us to set our minds on things above. If our minds and hearts are consumed with the goodies of this world, we may develop the "curse God and die" mentality — especially if we lose what we treasure most. I was guilty of treasuring an earthly relationship more than the one with my Heavenly Father. To this day, I have to remind myself to love deeply but hold loosely. In the early stages of his loss, Job firmly set his mind on the goodness of God. He held things loosely. Regardless if he lost the gifts from God, Job wouldn't curse the God he loved and served. His heart wasn't divided; it was steadfast.

Psalm 112:7 (NASB) tells us, "He will not fear evil tidings; His heart is steadfast, trusting in the LORD." 1 Corinthians 15:58 (NKJV) reinforces the truth: "Therefore, my beloved brethren, be steadfast, immovable, always abounding in the work of the Lord, knowing that your labor is not in vain in the Lord." And Hebrews 3:14 extols perseverance: "For we have become partakers of Christ if we hold the beginning of our confidence steadfast to the end."

NASA reports if a spacecraft lifting from the earth to the moon veers off even two percent at takeoff, it will miss the moon by 11,000 miles. If our hearts and minds are off even a smidgeon from the truth of who God is, what we speak will be as far off as well. Remember Job's friends? Their hearts, minds, and mouths were far off — and they grossly missed the target of ministering to Job when they spoke. This is a core life lesson to note. If what we think and speak to others varies from the heart and Word of God, we will miss the mark of real ministry. We must remain steadfast to the truth of who God is.

What would happen if members of The Queen's Guard at Buckingham Palace abandoned their steadfast positions? Thieves could wreak havoc in the palace. The lives of The Royal Family could be cut short.

If left unguarded, the same thing can happen to our hearts, minds, and mouths. Satan's ultimate goal is to sneak thoughts in our minds to kill, steal, and destroy our lives — and the lives of others. He wants our thoughts to take us captive, to make us his hostages.

BACK TO EDEN

When Adam and Eve walked and communed in the Garden of Eden with God, they were captivated and protected by Him. Their thoughts about God were pure. Their hearts were captivated by His love. The day Eve listened to Satan changed her life forever. Her mind believed the lie Satan whispered. Eve believed God wasn't as good as she had originally thought. Her heart felt cheated by God. She opened her heart and mind to the lies of Satan. She opened her mouth to eat, but ate more than fruit that day. She swallowed a lie that cost her dearly.

I often repeat this quote to myself: "Don't believe everything you think." If Eve had believed what God said instead of what Satan told her, child birthing would have been a different experience. She wouldn't have lost the paradise home she had once enjoyed. Her children would've loved each other. The list could continue for pages.

A.W. Tozer once said he didn't talk to the devil; he talked back to the devil. He wasn't a man who allowed Satan to feed him a sales pitch of lies. He quoted Scripture to ward off this relentless enemy. When Satan came to test Jesus in the wilderness, Jesus responded with Scripture. He guarded Himself with the Word of God. Eventually Satan fled, for the Word of God is far more powerful than the ruler of this world could ever be.

You and I must arm ourselves with God's Word. It is more protective than any Palace Guard. We are wise to memorize the Word of God as a tactical measure against the enemy. When we can verbally assault the lies trying to make entry into our minds and hearts, we become victorious. Left unguarded, we are easy targets for false beliefs to take up residence. As believers, we cannot be possessed by the devil, but false beliefs can consume us and take up space Truth should occupy. **We must** seek the Word of God and speak the Word of God.

Jeremiah 29:13 (NKJV) tells us, "You will seek Me and find Me, when you search for Me with all your heart." And Psalm 119:10 sets a golden example for us to follow: "With my whole heart I seek you; let me not wander from your commandments!" Do you see the connection here? If we seek God with a whole heart, we will find Him. We will find the right path. Our words will be congruent with our walk — protected by the very Word of God.

MOMENTS IN THE MIRROR

CHAPTER 11

1. What is the function of the soul on a day to day basis?

2. Have you ever realized the impact of your soul in relation to your behavior?

3. Understanding the significance of thinking, feeling, and doing/saying, what changes do you need to make in your life?

4. What thoughts seem to take you captive?

5. How do you combat the lies of the enemy?

6. Would you say you are more proactive against lies or more susceptible to being taken captive?

7. Is memorizing Scripture part of your Christian life?

"MIRROR, MIRROR"

If my heavenly Father paid such a high price to redeem me,

why should I continue to condemn myself?

Who can forget the famous line from the book *Snow White*? "Mirror, mirror on the wall, who's the fairest of them all?" It was a daunting question — one that mesmerized a wicked queen. Each day, the mirror spoke the only answer this woman wanted to hear: the fairest person in the land was none other than herself.

Why would a queen who sat exalted on a throne need to ask such a lowly question day after day? She was insecure. She quizzed the mirror to calm her soul. The queen held a position of high honor, but she suffered from a lack of identity. We are not told why she was so insecure, but from personal experience, I know that the words spoken by others — especially ones uttered by those close to us during childhood years — dramatically affect self-perception and life view.

HAMSTER WHEEL LIVING

When I was growing up, my family was ensnarled in anger, alcoholism, verbal and physical abuse, along with other dysfunctions that left me emotionally crippled. My self-esteem was so low I questioned my very existence for living. I also had an abject fear of God and the afterlife because I was constantly told any infraction deserved harsh punishment. At a young age, my goal was to be a good girl, to get through the day without making anyone mad — and without making any mistakes.

School was the one place I believed I could excel. Like a hamster on a wheel, I manically made my way through academic and extracurricular activities. I kept trying to amount to something. I desperately desired to make my parents proud. I wanted my teachers to think highly of me. And I practically sweated blood to be popular with my peers.

All this striving was exhausting. For every ten compliments I received, just one negative remark sent me on a downward spiral. Then I had to crawl out of the ditch of degradation to climb back on the hamster wheel, which was getting harder and harder to spin. The lies I heard and believed about myself made for horrific self-talk.

As I matured in age, I carried with me all the lies and acidic words spoken by others. I became living proof that when you inhale negativity, you exhale negativity. Sometimes, I playfully jested about those negative comments in an effort to prove that words could not hurt me. I may have appeared confident, but I was a shaking mess on the inside. A failing marriage signaled deep trouble. No amount of striving to do or be better was working. When I looked in my cracked mirror, I didn't need to ask, "Who's the fairest, smartest, skinniest, wittiest, most loved person in the world?" I knew the answer: anyone but me. I labeled myself, "the victim."

I needed help — and God led me to the most amazing place: Grace Ministries International and Scott Brittin, my counselor. This wise man immediately recognized what damaging years of acidic words and negative thinking had caused. He also noted my desperate desire to be healed. He certainly had his work cut out for him!

First, we carefully unpacked the piles of suitcases stuffed with my smelly past. This took quite some time. Over the years, I had packed layer after layer of festering hurt, and I had filled deep pockets with rotting lies. It was not a pretty sight — but a necessary one.

Next, we opened the Word of God to see if what I had learned and thought about myself matched up. We discarded everything that wasn't truth. We ended up tossing out pretty much everything, including the luggage cases. It felt like my whole life had been spent heading to the baggage carousel daily and hauling off as I much as I could carry. My initial intention for counseling was to learn how to carry all those suitcases while keeping the hamster wheel spinning. My false belief was that if I mastered this acrobatic feat, everyone would be happy and love me. I thank God for the heavy weight of all that baggage because it finally led me to get the help I needed to bring that pile of battered luggage to God, who had the perfect place for it: the foot of the cross.

The truth I discovered after sorting through and eventually tossing all that baggage was that in God's eyes, I was worth the price of Jesus Christ dying to pay for my sins. God didn't require perfection or high achievements to deem me lovable, nor did He belittle me for failure. He loved me unconditionally — even on days when I didn't make the good-girl cut. I learned that God is my advocate, not my accuser. I stepped off the hamster wheel and into a new life.

Hamster-wheel living was something I designed for myself. My

Creator wanted me to rest in Him, to abide under the Shadow of the Almighty — a place of safety and refuge. I claimed a new title for myself: daughter of the King Most High. No longer would I carry the victim banner. I discovered that God didn't call me names like fatso, idiot, jerk, or a host of other demeaning terms. These self-applied labels didn't honor the One who created me. Because of His love for me, He didn't want me to call myself those names either. If my Heavenly Father paid such a high price to redeem me, why should I continue to condemn myself? Nothing profitable occurs when we demean ourselves.

Best-selling author Seth Godin states, "People don't believe what you tell them. They rarely believe what you show them. They often believe what their friends tell them. They always believe what they tell themselves."[xiv]

Because Mr. Godin's statement is so often accurate, my counselor showed me how to adopt an entirely new vocabulary about myself. He also taught me the skill of mentally erasing negative words others said about me — and to forgive them for those words. I'm learning not to retaliate mentally or verbally the way I did in the past. Screaming, sarcasm, rude retorts, jesting with an edge of sting, manipulative words, false apologies, and fake excuses all needed to go.

Have I completely obliterated these verbal patterns? No! Am I working on surrendering them as they crop up? Yes!

Another important counseling session taught me to stop the train filled with anyone shouting (or even hinting) lies about me. My plumb line is the Word of God and the heart of God. If He doesn't speak or hold the same opinions of me as my accusers, then I must teach them a new way to relate to me — or I need to conduct them off my train. I have to teach others how to treat me, speak to me, and love me. I'm not advocating dismissing everyone who doesn't applaud or esteem me. I am reminding myself that disrespectful behavior from anyone is not acceptable, including me.

In 2 Corinthians 3:18 (NKJV) we are told, "But we all, with unveiled face, beholding as in a mirror the glory of the Lord, are being transformed into the same image from glory to glory, just as by the Spirit of the Lord." The mirror I look into reminds me I am being transformed daily into His likeness. I haven't arrived, but I'm slowly being changed. That brings me joy more than words can begin to express.

There are days when glancing into a mirror produces echoes from the past. The echoes condemn my imperfections, enhance my troubled areas, and seek to derail me for the day. If I don't denounce the echoes, they become roars. I can act as a lion that turns on itself. At this point, I have to choose truth – what does God see in me? What does God think about me? If I need to change any areas in my life, the Holy Spirit spotlights (not condemns) what needs correcting. Confession and correction leads to life change. Condemnation rarely does.

20/20 is a term used for perfect or clear vision. God sees us with a clear and a completed view. We may look in the mirror and pick out flaws which incapacitate us. But the One who created us sees us covered by the blood of His Son. Isaiah 61:10 (NLT) captures it best, "I am overwhelmed with joy in the LORD my God! For he has dressed me with the clothing of salvation and draped me in a robe of righteousness. I am like a bridegroom in his wedding suit or a bride with her **jewels**." What a beautiful image to behold.

Looking in the mirror with God's eyes will restore life and joy when defeat and depression distort truth. The mirrors at a carnival distort our images and we laugh. Satan desires to distort our mirrors with lies and guilt – no laughing, just tears of regret. We either chose to see ourselves through God's eyes or the Satan's. Deut.30:19-20(ESV), "I call **heaven and earth** to witness against you today, that I have set before you life and death, blessing and curse. Therefore choose life, that you and your offspring may live, loving the LORD your God, obeying his voice and holding fast to him, for he is your life and length of days…"

My counselor assigned me a difficult task. He asked me to keep looking in the mirror until I heard words of affirmation from my Creator. This took me quite some time. When I embraced truth from His Word, memorized it, and repeated it to drown out the lies, I embraced who He made me. Please hear me; this is not a onetime assignment. Forty years later, I am still making Him my mirror manager.

MOMENTS IN THE MIRROR

CHAPTER 12

1. What personal messages did you accumulate while growing up?

2. Who had the most influence on you and how did the influence impact you?

3. Do you carry any baggage that needs to be discarded?

4. What does your self- talk sound like?

5. What words or phrases about yourself do not line up with God's thoughts about you?

6. Are you in the habit of name calling others in a negative light?

7. What changes do you need to make in view of what God says about you?

BUT GOD

Christ died for your freedom, not for you to live in bondage to sinful behavior.

Without fail, human lions roar every day – in our homes, workplaces, churches, and public places. Think about the roaring lions that prowl in your life, the ones who chase after you, wounding you with savage words. Are you tired of running? Are you bone-dead weary of trying to escape the razor-sharp teeth that rip you apart?

Maybe you've learned some coping mechanism to mute a lion's terrifying roar and piercing words. Perhaps, because the lion is a repeat visitor, you've chosen a weapon, either mentally or verbally, to defend yourself against attacks.

Perhaps, the roar of the lion that once intimidated you has become a drone. You've lost all respect and respond with disgust.

Or maybe you've simply given up, too exhausted to take another step. Personal descriptive adjectives that once included vivacious, cheerful, lively, walks with a spring in the step, and happy-go-lucky have been replaced by fearful, withdrawn, depressed, and hesitant. A counselor's worst-case scenario is a client who no longer cares. Even the smallest fraction of anger implies there's still some fight left in a person. However, disconnected eyes are the kiss of death in restoring the victim of a lion.

Here's another possibility: *The vicious lion many fear is* **you**. Roaring the loudest has always worked for you. But now, for some reason, you find no pleasure in watching the fear of your victims. You see them run when you approach. Their defeated faces gnaw at you each night. Those who once esteemed you, now turn away. You're no longer considered the authority, just the one who roars loudly and demands obedience.

Proverbs 20:2 (NKJV) tells us, "The wrath of the king is like the roaring of a lion." Can you hear the harsh echo of your roaring, bouncing off the walls of your life and the hearts of your victims? Matthew Henry in his King's English commentary captures the life and legacy of a roaring lion this way:

> "See here, formidable kings are, and what a terror
> they strike upon those they are angry with. Their fear, with
> which (especially when they are absolute and their will is a
> law) they keep their subjects in awe, is as the roaring of a

lion, which is very dreadful to the creatures he preys upon, and makes them tremble so that they cannot escape from him. Those princes that rule by wisdom and love rule like God himself, and bear his image; but those that rule merely by terror, and with a high hand, do but rule like a lion in the forest, with a brutal power. *Oderint, dum metuant*—Let them hate, provided they fear. How unwise therefore those are that quarrel with them that are angry at them, and so provoke them to anger. They sin against their own lives. Much more do those do so that provoke the King of kings to anger. *Nemo me impune lacesset*—No one shall provoke me with impunity."[xv]

Do you hear what this Bible scholar of old is saying? Those who rule with a roar strike up fear, not love or allegiance. A king, much like a lion, has the capacity to sentence his subject to either life or death. He opens his mouth and consequences ensue. Wise people have a healthy perspective about obeying the law and corresponding respect for those who enforce it. However, if a king or authority subverts the law to his own advantage at the expense of others, he will not escape judgment himself. Proverbs 14:28 (NIV) sums up these truths this way: "A large population is a king's glory, but without subjects a prince is ruined."

If you esteem yourself as a leader but have no one following you, re-evaluate your leadership style. If you've used a loud roar to dominate, manipulate, or control the people around you, your legacy is likely in ruins. Here are two questions to ask yourself: *What will my family and friends have to say about me in my eulogy? Will I leave this earth with people mourning my loss — or dancing on my tombstone?* If your answer makes you cringe, then changes need to be made. Christ centered counseling changed my life.

LETTING GO

What are some practical steps for renouncing lion mentality? Honesty and transparency are major factors to facilitate healing. If your life consists of one broken relationship after another there's a reason. Continuing to deny the truth will impede spiritual and personal growth. Be willing to admit what others have remarked about you, either to your face or behind your back. Only the truth will set you free. Christ died for your freedom – not for you to live in bondage to sinful behavior.

If there's an accumulation of wounds from your past, bring them to the Healer. Scars emerge in various ways. Bitterness, rage, and anger rarely stay below the surface. They are internally and externally destructive. Anger management classes may help for awhile, but true healing comes from anger eradication – not management! If dominating others is an issue, understand you're out of control, not in control. You may have subordinates but not loyal followers. Perhaps through blood, sweat, and tears you've made it to the top. You swipe your claws at anyone who draws near to your throne. The crown of entitlement doesn't look good on anyone. Neither does the green eyed monster of jealousy.

The list of emotional wounds and scarring is extensive. The great news is that healing is possible. A prescription is found in Isaiah 53:5(NIV), "But he was pierced for our transgressions, he was crushed for our iniquities; the punishment that brought us peace was on him, and by his wounds we are healed." Your past doesn't have to define your present or your future. Don't leave this life regretting how you treated another human life.

A POWERFUL CONNECTION

In the midst of roaring lions and their victims, two powerful words linked together speak clearly above the fray: **But God.** I have personally experienced the powerful truth found in these two words. A lion slowly crept into my life step by step — until I was under full attack. Before long, I found myself in a vicious cycle of retreating in fear; fighting back with Scripture, logic, and witnesses; silent standoff's; being eaten alive by my own anger; pretending to be dead; arguing with God; and last but not least, prayer.

In my argumentative phase, two words spoken with accusing fervor repeatedly flew from my mouth: "But God!" I spoke them as if He were oblivious to my situation. I couldn't understand why God wasn't slaying my lion. This mindset was wreaking havoc wherever I went.

One day, while prayerfully talking to God, I screamed out the infamous, "But God!" for the umpteenth time. And then I stopped mid-scream and asked myself: *Did the two words, But God, appear anywhere in Scripture?* I went on a hunt. My concordance listed 584 verses with inexact matches and 40 verses with the exact match of "But God." What I discovered was astounding! When situations seemed impossible and people feared God had forgotten them, two words appeared: ***But God.***

After Noah built the ark, gathered all the animals, herded them on the ark, and closed the doors, he waited for 150 days. Five months with family and animals — all during an extended storm. I imagine the days were beastly long and so were the nights. We're not privy to any conversations Noah had with God, but I'm certain he wondered how long the storm would last. Then, in Genesis 8:1 we see these words: "**But God** remembered Noah." After the storm, which seemed endless, God revealed Himself — and a whole new life began.

The biblical account of Joseph ranks at the top of my favorite "But God" list. His story begins in Genesis 37. Although adored by his father, Joseph was hated by his brothers. They all but killed him, choosing instead to sell him into slavery. From that point, his life veered with various twists and turns. He was accused of rape (though innocent) and stayed in prison seven long years. After his release and promotion to a place of power, Joseph experienced a blast from the past: His brothers appeared before him to beg for grain during a famine. Fifteen years had passed, and they did not recognize their little brother. But Joseph recognized them.

Chapters 42 through 50 keep you on the edge of your seat as you anticipate what Joseph would do to his siblings. In his youth, the brothers had been fierce lions. Jealous and cynical, they had mocked Joseph as a dreamer and abused him. The story ends with one of the greatest verses in the Bible, Genesis 50:20. Joseph looked at his former lions and comforted them with these words, "But as for you, you meant evil against me; **But God** meant it for good." Joseph, the brother once a victim, emerged as the victor – both personally and within the ranks of family and his country.

Victims are not meant to stay victims. The enemy comes to steal, kill, and destroy. When I embarked on my Bible search of "but God" references, I came to the conclusion my anger and defeated mentality trumped my trust in God. If He could stop the rain for Noah, deliver Joseph from numerous plights, and rescue countless others from their personal lions, He could deliver me. I exchanged my anguished cries of "but God...." for the powerful links "But God." As I repeated this phrase on a daily bases, an invisible chain link fence protected me from my lion.

Psalm 91:9-16 (ESV) describe the power and protection of the fence:

9 Because you have made the LORD your dwelling place-- the Most High, who is my refuge-- **10** no evil shall be allowed to befall you, no plague come near your tent. **11** For he will command his angels concerning you to guard you in all your ways. **12** On their hands they will bear you up, lest you strike your foot against a stone. **13** You will tread on the lion and the adder; the young lion and the serpent you will trample underfoot. **14** "Because he holds fast to me in love, I will deliver him; I will protect him, because he knows my name. **15** When he calls to me, I will answer him; I will be with him in trouble; I will rescue him and honor him. **16** With long life I will satisfy him and show him my salvation."

The choice to stay in a victim mentality denies the power of an almighty God. The lion may continue roaring, but as believers in Christ, we are more than conquerors who can walk in victory. He has given us the power to overcome! We must choose to walk in resurrection power, not buckle in defeat.

But God knows about lions. As Creator, He made each of us in His image. He didn't make us to be roaring lions, nor did He make us to be victims of them. Neither of these roles glorifies Him. Our identity is in Him. It is in Him that we live and move and have our being (Acts 17:28).

As you reach the end of this book, do you identify as a roaring lion? Or do you identify as the victim of one? The source of redemption is the same for both: Cry out to the "***But God***" of the Bible. He rescues and He resurrects those caught in either of these traps. As the resurrected Savior, He is capable of resurrecting roaring lions from despicable behavior. He is also capable of resurrecting victims from the mouths of vicious lions.

Christian music artist Nicol Sponberg wrote the song "Resurrection," which captures the heart of *When Lions Roar*:

> "I'm at a loss for words, there's nothing to say.
> I sit in silence, wondering what led me to this place.
> How did my heart become so lifeless and cold?
> Where did the passion go?
>
> When all my efforts seem like chasing wind,
> I've used up all my strength and there's nothing left to give
> I've lost the feeling and I'm numb to the core
> I can't fake it anymore.
>
> chorus:
> Here I am at the end; I'm in need of resurrection.
> Only You can take this empty shell and raise it from the dead.
> What I've lost to the world, what seems far beyond redemption;
> You can take the pieces in Your hand and make me whole again,
> again.

You speak and all creation falls to its knees.
You raise Your hand and calm the waves of the raging sea.
You have a way of turning winter to spring.
Make something beautiful out of all this suffering."[xvi]

Whether you're a roaring lion or the victim of one, the King of kings can resurrect you into a new life. He desires to show you mercy and grace so that in turn you may live and speak mercy and grace to others.

May you seek Him and find Him, my friend. God bless you on your journey!

MOMENTS IN THE MIRROR

CHAPTER 13

1. Are you the lion or the victim?

2. How did you relate to the depiction of a lion roaring?

3. How did you relate to the feelings of being the victim?

4. Have you ever reached the point of hopelessness in a relationship?

5. Are you in need of resurrection from the only One who can breathe life back into your soul?

6. What changes do you need to make after reading *When Lions Roar?*

ABOUT THE AUTHOR

Dawn Mooring is a certified counselor, trained by Grace Ministries International, and the American Association of Christian Counselors, specializing in women's ministry.

A gifted speaker and Bible teacher, Mooring has taught Sunday school and small group Bible studies for more than twenty years. She is the author of two Bible studies and has been published in _The Upper Room_, _christiandevotions.us_, several blogspots, and a church devotional _Watercolors_.

Mooring has appeared on the television shows "Atlanta Live" and "Friends and Neighbors." Currently she is a co-host on The Christian View aired weekly on WATC, an Atlanta based television station and in partnership with SkyAngel 2, and Parable Network, reaching 21 million homes.

Dawn and her husband Mark live near Woodstock, Georgia. They have two married daughters and three granddaughters. Her passion is teaching others to know, to love, and to live God's Word.

To find out more about Dawn visit her website: www.dawnmooring.com.

ENDNOTES

[i] http://wikianswers.com/Q/whydoesthelionroar#ixzz28T46MSC6

[ii] Unknown source

[iii]James MacDonald, *Lord, Change My Attitude* (Chicago: Moody Publishers, 2001/2008), p.26.

[iv]Phineas Camp Headley, *Miriam* (Miller, Orton & Mulligan: Blue Letter Bible. 26, Feb 2011. 2012. 10, October 2012).

[v] David Guzik, *Study Guide for Numbers 20* (Enduring Word: Blue Letter Bible. 7, July 2006. 2012. 13, October 2012).

[vi] Ibid

[vii]Boyd Bailey, *Wisdom Hunters: Self Flattery* (http://bit.ly/bQHNIE)

[viii]Kyle Idleman, *Not a Fan* (Grand Rapids, MI: Zondervan, 2011), p. 163-164.

[ix] *The MacArthur Study Bible*, Ed. John Mac Arthur (Nashville, TN: Thomas Nelson, Inc., 1997), p. 740.

[x] http://www.goodreads.com/book/show/210935.Intimacy

[xi] Larry Crabb, *The Safest Place on Earth* (Nashville, TN: Word Publishing/Thomas Nelson, 1999) p. 4.

[xii] http://www.walk-this-way.com/confession.htm (Cody Smith, "Confess Your Sins to One Another.")

[xiii]Ibid

[xiv] http://www.goodreads.com/author/quotes/1791.Seth_Godin

[xv]*Matthew Henry Commentary on Proverbs 20*, Blue Letter Bible. 1, March 1996. 2013. 26, July 2013.

[xvi] Heimermann, Mark and Sponberg, Nicol. *"Resurrection."* Franklin, TN. Fun Attic Music, Curb Songs, 2004. (Copyright by Permission)

40452993R00066

Made in the USA
Charleston, SC
06 April 2015